I am from the house of Estrada

I am older than Velasco and to the king I owe nothing.

HERALDIC MOTTO

ALEJANDRO

Written by

Alejandro Carbajal Estrada

ISBN-13: 978-0692329771
ISBN-10: 0692329773

ISBN-13: 978-1505279627
ISBN-10: 1505279623

ANTI CHRIST ENDOWMENTS, LOS ANGELES

©ACE 2014 ©ACE 2016
ALL RIGHTS RESERVED. NO PART OF THIS BOOK MAY BE REPRODUCED OR TRANSMITTED IN ANY FORM OR BY ANY MEANS WITHOUT WRITTEN PERMISSION FROM THE AUTHOR.

"We, the Noble Knights
of the Roundtable,
Rest our Shields,
Against the Heads Mounted
on the walls of this
Great Hall."

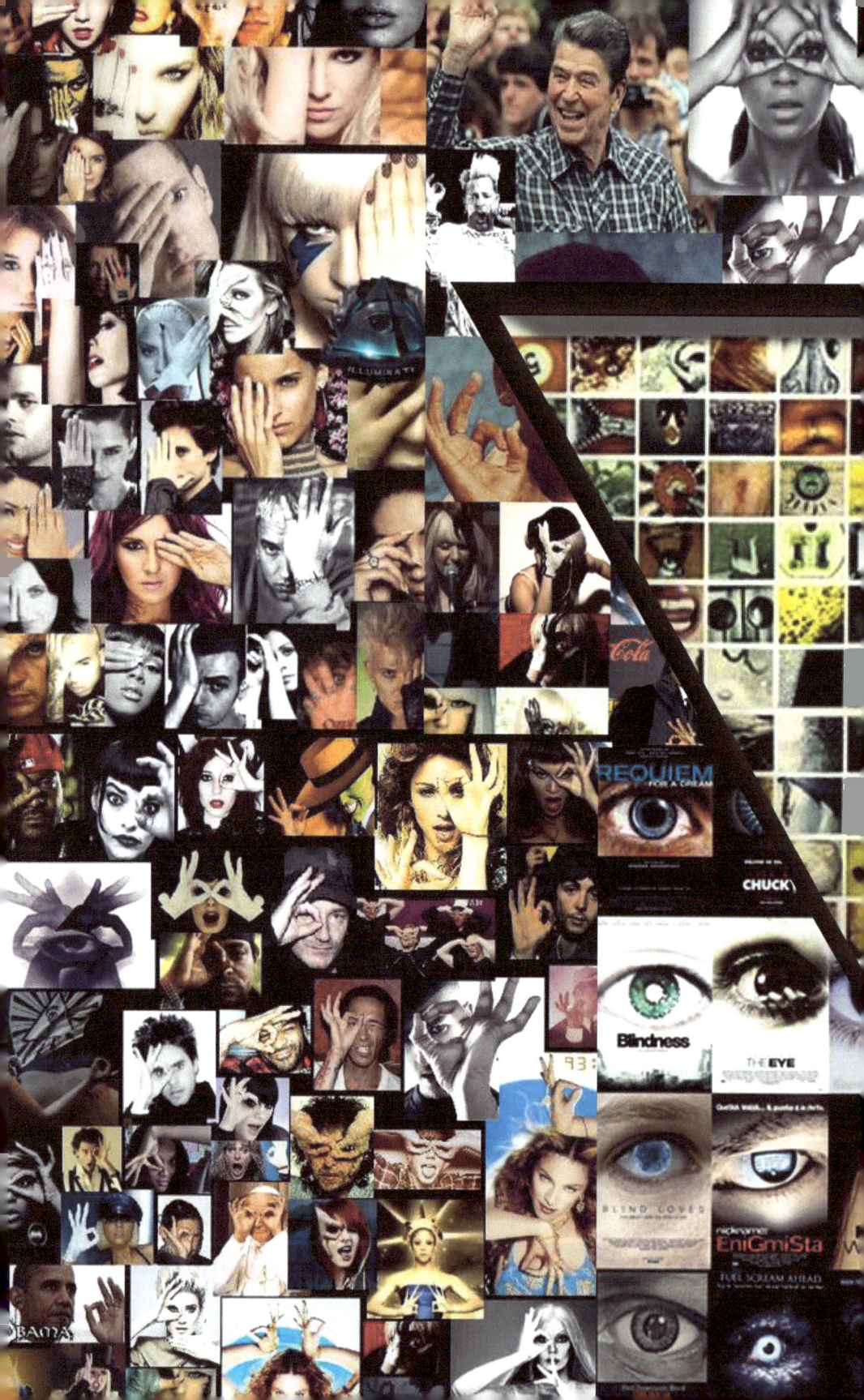

Table of Contents

Foreword   12

Alice's Hungry Hole   46
   Long Pork   54
   The Confrontation   61

The Wizard and the Emerald City   68
   Robin Williams   84

Mark Combs   118

LETTERS AND MEMOS   132
MEMO TO LASD   137
MEMO TO RIVERSIDE COUNTY DA   146
MEMO TO MARIN COUNTY   150
LETTER TO CHAPMAN UNIVERSITY   154
LETTERS TO WIKIPEDIA FOUNDATION   156
WIKIMEDIA SUPPORT TEAM   162
LETTER TO WIKIPEDIA LEGAL DEPARTMENT   164

ACKNOWLEDGMENTS   168

AFTERWORD   174

```
                                    ┌─────────────────────┐
                                    │   575 Anton Blvd.   │
                                    └─────────────────────┘
┌──────────────────┐
│  RWR Homes Inc.  │─┤
└──────────────────┘                 ┌──────────────────────────┐
                                     │ 16461 Sherman Way #350   │
                                     │      Van Nuys, CA        │
                                     └──────────────────────────┘

                                    ┌─────────────────────┐        ┌──────────────────────────┐        ┌──────────────────────────┐
                                    │  Skyline 32 Tustin  │        │ Shen Mary and Family LLC │        │  15660 Tustin Village #A │
                                    │   558 Sacremento    │────────│    943 Kingsly Drive     │────────│                          │
                                    │      SF, CA         │        │                          │        └──────────────────────────┘
┌────────────────────────┐          └─────────────────────┘        └──────────────────────────┘
│  Washington Mutual     │─┤
│     Scottsdale, AZ     │          ┌─────────────────────┐        ┌──────────────────────────┐        ┌──────────────────────────┐
└────────────────────────┘          │       Rreef         │        │    RWR Associates, LLC   │        │    560 Sacremento        │
                                    │   640 Sacremento    │────────│                          │────────│       SF, CA             │
                                    └─────────────────────┘        └──────────────────────────┘        └──────────────────────────┘

┌────────────────────────┐                                         ┌──────────────────────────┐
│    RWR Associates      │          ┌─────────────────────┐        │        John King        │        ┌──────────────────────────┐
│    DBA Starlink.net    │──────────│    Vincent Wynn     │────────│ kyawwynn@hotmail.com     │────────│   John and Cindy McCain  │
└────────────────────────┘          └─────────────────────┘        │ I.P. address 66.81.190.193│       └──────────────────────────┘
                                                                   └──────────────────────────┘

                                    ┌─────────────────────┐        ┌──────────────────────────┐
                                    │ 847 Hammond Street  │        │     Kathryn Laterza      │        ┌──────────────────────────┐
                                    │                     │        │      Health4Life.net     │        │      Cindy McCain        │
┌────────────────────────┐          └─────────────────────┘        └──────────────────────────┘        └──────────────────────────┘
│  Michael Goss Estate   │─┤
└────────────────────────┘          ┌─────────────────────┐        ┌──────────────────────────┐        ┌──────────────────────────┐
                                    │     Loz Feliz       │        │   John and Karen King    │        │    John and Cndy McCain  │
                                    └─────────────────────┘        └──────────────────────────┘        └──────────────────────────┘
```

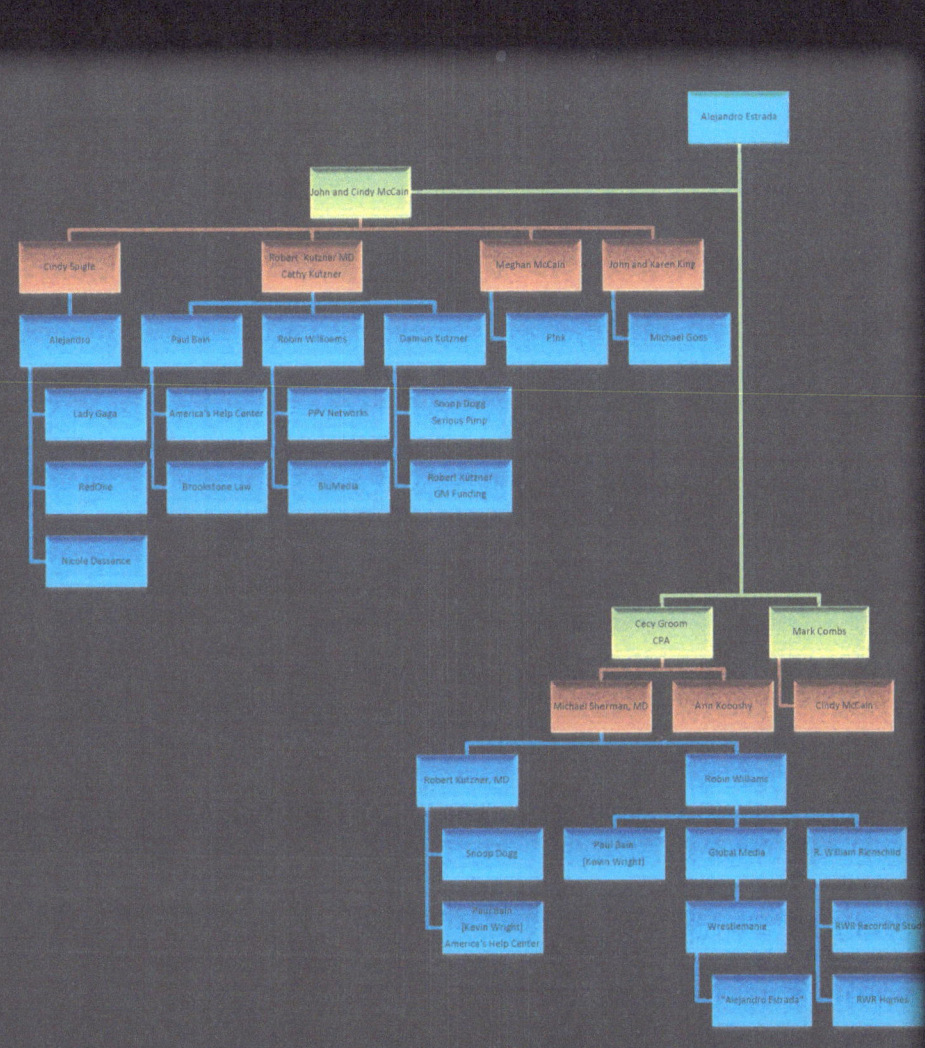

Foreword

Secrets only harm those who keep them.

"It" does not have a name. "It" is intangible and invisible, yet universal and something everyone knows, regardless of language or cultural difference. "It," is the mirror opposite of Celebrity and if there is a place called Hell, that would be it. "It" is a worst-nightmare-comes-true for all affected parties because it is an anomaly that capsizes the balance of power. The tables turn, the illusionists controlling global affairs become disadvantaged. Those puppet masters find themselves indebted for a value that money will never pay off. They become overwhelmed by the stress and in a panic-stricken attempt motivated by vanity, they tailspin towards an unavoidable demise. It will be too late when they realize that every action they implemented to regain the advantage, only dug them a deeper hole of debt. This time, however, the debt is well within their ability to afford. Paying it will cost them more than just money. Not only will it be suicide, but it will jeopardize the livelihood of their future generations; in settling this debt, they will give open acknowledgment to their secrets. This cabal faces defeat because nothing in life is free, and every wrong decision has its consequence.

A L E J A N D R O

Nonetheless, their struggle for self-preservation blinds them, and the collective realizes the end is upon them. The longer they avoid facing accountability, the worse things become. But these people are not lay persons ignorant of mystic science; they are Gnostic masters well versed in secret knowledge. They understand these phenomena better than anyone else. So much in fact, they structure their entire lives around it, which consequently seals their fate and potentially the fate of the world at large. Having this awareness, they become frantic and disoriented as if they've just committed murder without securing a safe way of disposing of their evidence.

The worst course of actions becomes as logical as digging graves in flower gardens (so to speak). What materializes is the attempt to dilute the crime and the easiest avenue in which to do so, is via mainstream and alternative media. Fifty years ago, this may have worked however in the current age of the Internet this creates content and as content accumulates, so does the relevance of the information. Consequently, one's likeness is seen throughout the world, and one's name becomes a household icon. One's words become plagiarized. One's life becomes exploited. Except, one is helpless and cannot do anything about it because unlike other celebrities, they did not seek fame. Nor, did they sign a contract to acquire fame

Ultimately, "it" is living in a world that does not want you part of it. All the while, eagerly jumping over swine just to get on your back. As if the weight of the world balancing on your shoulders, was not enough, it becomes the cross for your crucifixion. Meanwhile, the sound of clamor crescendos towards complete chaos. Slanderous words intended with malice pierce like daggers.

A L E J A N D R O

"Delusional" "Crazy" "Worthless" "Nobody" "Ugly" and asking questions like *"Who does he think he is?"* From that whirlwind, a sort of celebrity begins to take shape. The world population believes you are a fictional character, and only a select few know otherwise. A group so elite, membership is reserved for the key figures directly involved in the conspiracy. Welcome, to my prison; my fate and perhaps my destiny. I am blacklisted by the Associated Press because multimedia conglomerates are controlled by profit. Public servants are serving a society controlled by money, and the result is a legalized form of prostitution wherein the sex is a filthy free for all. A society driven by greed and criminal acquisition is without morality, headed for failure. The United States of America is now past the point of no return.

When I published *Pandora, her Box and her Daddy's Curse* in 2012, the Truth Movement was sparked except the media diverted attention by censoring my message. In my search for answers, a veil of deception was lifted from my view exposing a cancerous growth within the government of the Vatican State. Then, divine intervention guided me to a document entitled "In Eminenti: The Papal Bull of Pope Clement XII." An altercation with the Catholic Church erupted, and less than six months later I had established myself as being a prophet equal to Moses.

A L E J A N D R O

I brought " In Eminenti" to the Ministry of Divine Faith, in August 2012, and demanded a worldwide Inquisition against Freemasonry. Then, after being ignored, I sent it to the Office of the Pope. Again, I was dismissed, and that caused me to become incensed. In response, I threatened two Bishops, a Cardinal, and I gave Pope Benedict XVI an ultimatum. In a press release dated October 16, 2012, I gave the Pope a directive and specified that if that directive were not adhered to, there would be catastrophic consequences. I elaborated how a group of children would meet their fate after being led in, to a rock quarry.

> *"...the flock [will be led] down a rocky ridge of which, none will be able to climb up from."*

The press release communicated very precisely that if the Vatican failed to declare an Inquisition, it would be received by G-D, as an act of defiance. I then prophesied. The world bared witness. I stated that if the Pope failed to enforce Vatican Law, then the blood of those innocent children would be on his hands; because no child would walk out alive from that rock quarry.

> *" The need for urgency is because one, two maybe three more steps and the human race will be balancing itself on the edge of a flooded quarry; and then I will not be a matter of if, but when the tender hooves of G-D's lamb lose their footing on the slippery slanted rocks of the quarry; at which point nothing will save us from the Beast called Freemasonry."*

In closing, I expressed a profound regret for being the harbinger and stated how the event in the rock quarry would foreshadow an abomination of desolation because the following tragedy would dwarf the catastrophe from the first event.

Mourners bury family killed in Guatemala quake

BY MIKE MCDONALD

SAN CRISTOBAL CUCHO, Guatemala   Fri Nov 9, 2012 8:14pm EST

1 OF 6. People carry to the cemetery the coffin of one of the four members of the De Leon family, who were killed during a landslide triggered by a 7.4-magnitude earthquake, in El Recreo, in the outskirts of San Pedro Sacatepequez in the San Marcos region, about 250 km (155 miles) away of Guatemala City, November 9, 2012.
CREDIT: REUTERS/WILLIAM GULARTE

RELATED VIDEO

Guatemalan villagers mourn quake victims

RELATED NEWS

Guatemala scours for quake survivors, death toll

(Reuters) - Ivan Vasquez cried as he hunched over the 10 wooden caskets of his parents, six siblings and two cousins who were struck down in a rock quarry collapse caused by this week's powerful earthquake.

Vasquez was studying to take an accounting exam when the 7.4-magnitude quake struck on Wednesday, killing his entire immediate family as they dug in the quarry for material to reinforce the walls of their adobe home.

A L E J A N D R O

My prophecy came to fruition during a magnitude 7.4 earthquake in Guatemala on November 7, 2012. The entire Vazquez family was buried alive inside of a rock quarry; eight of the victims were children. That incident took place exactly according to my description, and it foreshadowed a far greater tragedy; the massacre at Sandy Hook Catholic Parish Elementary.

A month later, approximately twenty innocent children were murdered using government issued military grade firearms. The events of December 14, 2012, are unclear, crowded with convoluted details and discrepancies. According to the Associated Press, the principle was Monsignor Robert Weiss. The newly built school was torn down and rebuilt. Money was not an object, and the entire nation was blind to the reality. Evidence was destroyed by the reconstruction and months later, the Social Security Death Index indicated the gunman, Adam Lanza, died on December 13, 2012. When the public questioned this oversight, the record was "corrected" and now shows December 14, 2012.

However, no one caught the "error" regarding the place of death, because

[Death certificate image showing: State of Connecticut, Department of Public Health, Office of the Chief Medical Examiner, Certificate of Death for Adam Peter Lanza. Date of death: December 14, 2012, 11:00 AM. Date of birth: April 22 1992, Exeter NH. Residence: 36 Yogananda St, Sandy Hook, 06482, Fairfield County, Connecticut, Newtown. Father: Peter Lanza. Mother: Nancy Champion. Informant: Peter Lanza, Father, 100 Bartina Ln Stamford CT 06902. Place of death: Public School, 12 Dickinson Drive. Disposition: Linwood Crematory, Haverhill MA, 12/22/2012. Cause of death: Gunshot Wound of Head. Manner of death: Suicide. Date of injury: December 14, 2012, AM. Place of injury: School, Primary or Secondary. Location of injury: 12 Dickinson Dr., Sandy Hook, CT. Self Inflicted. Certifier: H. Wayne Carver, II, M.D., Chief Medical Examiner, Dec 16, 2012. Office of the Chief Medical Examiner, 11 Shuttle Road, Farmington, CT 06032-1939. Decedent's usual occupation: Never Worked. Signed by Debbie A. Aurelia, Registrar, 1-3-13.]

according to the Social Security Death Index, Adam Lanza died in the State of New Hampshire. According to Adam Lanza's death certificate, he died in the state of Connecticut. There was too much media coverage for there to have been an error. Everyone in the country knew the name Adam Lanza. December 14, 2012, fell on a Friday. Therefore, the records. In addition, I was able to uncover this document on a cached server. This record no longer exists.

> COMPLETED FORM TO YOUR LOCAL SOCIAL SECURITY OFFICE. The office is listed under U.S. Government agencies in your telephone directory or you may call Social Security at 1-800-772-1213 (TTY 1-800-325-0778). You may send comments on our time estimate above to: SSA, 6401 Security Blvd., Baltimore, MD 21235-6401. Send *only* comments relating to our time estimate to this address, not completed form.
>
> 1. NAME OF DECEASED: Adam P. Lanza
> 2. SOCIAL SECURITY NUMBER: 002-84-5443
> 3. DATE OF DEATH: 12/13/12
> 4. DATE OF BIRTH (if known): 4/22/92
> 5. Check (x) whether the deceased was: ☒ Male ☐ Female
> 6. NAME OF WIDOW OR WIDOWER (if known):
> 7. ADDRESS (No. and Street, P.O. Box) OF WIDOW OR WIDOWER (if known):

The handwriting matches this document, which was used to replace the previous one.

> **STATEMENT OF DEATH BY FUNERAL DIRECTOR**
>
> NAME OF DECEASED: Adam P. Lanza
> SOCIAL SECURITY NUMBER: 002-84-5443
>
> FOR SSA USE ONLY
>
> Please complete the items below, and return the form in the enclosed addressed, postage paid envelope. Your assistance and cooperation are appreciated.
>
> PRIVACY ACT/PAPERWORK ACT NOTICE: The information on this form is authorized by Section 404.715 and 404.720 of the Federal Regulations (20 CFR 404.715 and 404.720). While your response is voluntary, we need your assistance to make an accurate and timely determination concerning the death of the individual named above, and to determine if there are survivors who may be eligible for Social Security benefits.
>
> We may also use the information you give us when we match records by computer. Matching programs compare our records with those of other Federal, State or local government agencies. Many agencies may use matching programs to find or prove that a person qualifies for benefits paid by the Federal government. The law allows us to do this even if you do not agree to it.
>
> Explanations about these and other reasons why information you provide us may be used or given out are available in Social Security Offices. If you want to learn more about this, contact any Social Security Office.
>
> Paperwork Reduction Act Statement - This information collection meets the requirements of 44 U.S.C. § 3507, as amended by Section 2 of the Paperwork Reduction Act of 1995. You do not need to answer these questions unless we display a valid Office of Management and Budget control number. We estimate that it will take about 3.5 minutes to read the instructions, gather the facts, and answer the questions. SEND THE COMPLETED FORM TO YOUR LOCAL SOCIAL SECURITY OFFICE. The office is listed under U. S. Government agencies in your telephone directory or you may call Social Security at 1-800-772-1213 (TTY 1-800-325-0778). You may send comments on our time estimate above to: SSA, 6401 Security Blvd., Baltimore, MD 21235-6401. Send *only* comments relating to our time estimate to this address, not completed form.
>
> 1. NAME OF DECEASED: Adam P. Lanza
> 2. SOCIAL SECURITY NUMBER: 002-84-5443
> 3. DATE OF DEATH: 12/14/2012
> 4. DATE OF BIRTH (if known): 4/22/1992
> 5. Check (x) whether the deceased was: ☒ Male ☐ Female

I have exposed too much corruption regarding the government's manipulation of death records. Any logical and sound-minded person should not blindly accept blatant errors such as these in any official record because these are not honest mistakes. A honest mistake does not require an entirely new document. The fact that a single document was destroyed automatically qualifies as a crime.

This is part of the reason I decided to make my private information public. There is no rationale to accept or overlook these crimes. I did not make my information public so that people would pity me. Just because I am a victim who is struggling to survive, living a life not worth living, exploited and slandered in the media, the last thing I need is to become someone's martyr. Consequently, the slander against me became the Great Expectation I have been trying to not just live up to, but to exceed. The best idea I came up with created so much cognitive dissonance, that everyone ignored it. I claimed to be the "Antichrist" because I needed a gimmick. Since I am an over-achieving perfectionist, that was the craziest idea that came to me. At that time I had found myself stuck inside of a Hunger Game, facing a grim quietus. I had nothing to lose.

But, the purpose of this book is to clarify the missing information in my first book because the truth is, I was clueless when I wrote *Pandora, Her Box, and Her Daddy's Curse*. All I knew then, was that bad people had locked me out of my house and they were squatting on my personal property. Even though I was able to prove Michael Goss had been murdered, I was not able to name the people who killed him; at least not by their real names.

A lot has happened in the last two years. There have been tremendous discoveries, and now I am able to identify the people responsible. As well as present the forensic evidence to prove it. When I tried to ask them for retribution, they have sought to have me killed. It was to be expected. They are evil. I have survived two fatal car accidents and a burning building. They are still trying and I am beginning to use their attempts as comedy relief. How hard could it be? They would starve to death if they had to earn their own living. So since bad people destroy truth, I decided to embrace it. Unfortunately, the world I lived in was anything but honest and the people in this world have too much social influence over the real world everyone else lives in. In the real world, I am just someone claiming to have known a dead porn director. I would be doing myself an injustice if I believe strangers are not judging me based on that one detail.

Therefore, I am evening the playing field by revealing pornography as the common denominator between me and my perpetrators. The difference is that Michael Goss produced legal pornography and I cannot say the same for the people who killed him. Somehow the Federal Bureau of Investigation condones it. The FBI destroys every request I have filed for an investigation. Well, of course, the FBI does not investigate itself. That should have been a no-brainer. For the record, Michael Goss was my boss. I was his personal assistant. He was murdered shortly after making the decision to name me as a beneficiary of his estate. Then, I was locked out of our house by strangers.

I claimed to be Michael Goss's domestic partner in order to gain an advantage over my perpetrators. Before working for Michael Goss, I had worked as a personal assistant to the Certified Public Accountant, Cecy Groom. In addition to being a CPA, Cecy Groom is a retired school board member with over twenty years of experience in public service; she even ran for congress twice. After auditing those files, I discovered evidence linking Cecy Groom to a suspected drug dealer, [Stefano Russo] connected to the West Hollywood gay bar MICKY'S.

A L E J A N D R O

I also found intimate photographs of Stefano Russo with Cindy McCain (Senator John McCain's wife) and Gloria Allred. Stefano's connection to MICKY'S is significant because MICKY'S employs a "Lady Gaga" impersonator that goes by the stage name "Judas Joe Manson."

ALEJANDRO

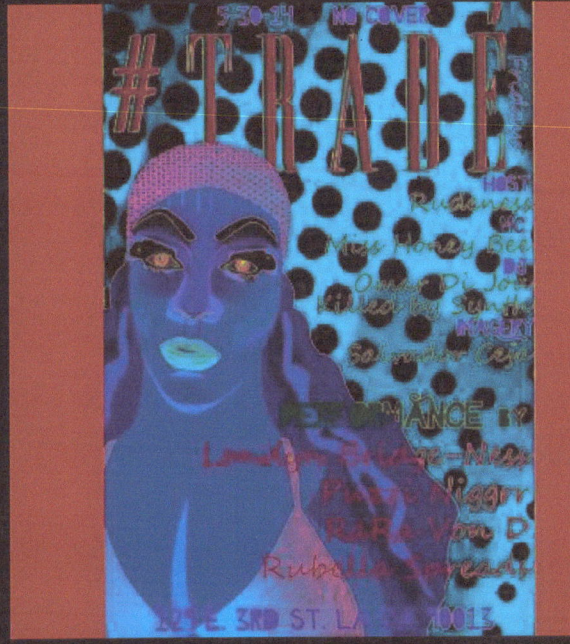

I have reason to suspect this individual of being the real Lady Gaga. To the best of my knowledge His name is Gabriel Codero an he requested that I not use these images.

A L E J A N D R O

However, it is public domain. Besides, how could I not use it—that could be the only public domain image showing Lady Gaga blocking his male genitalia during a photo shoot. According to American Express Bank, he opened an account using the name "Joseph Manson." I obtained this evidence because apparently, he is using my address in West Hollywood, as his mailing address. By doing so, he may have committed bank fraud; however, the authorities are protecting him. This seemingly innocent crime could be argued as terrorism except the Los Angeles Sheriffs and Federal Bureau of Investigation continue to ignore it. In total, this discovery gave me a substantial lead, and while examining Cecy's congressional files, I discovered a photograph of her with Zelda Williams (Robin Williams's daughter). Apparently, Robin Williams and Michael Aquino engaged a military psych-op to lead my investigation astray. However, by doing so, they brought me further on track.

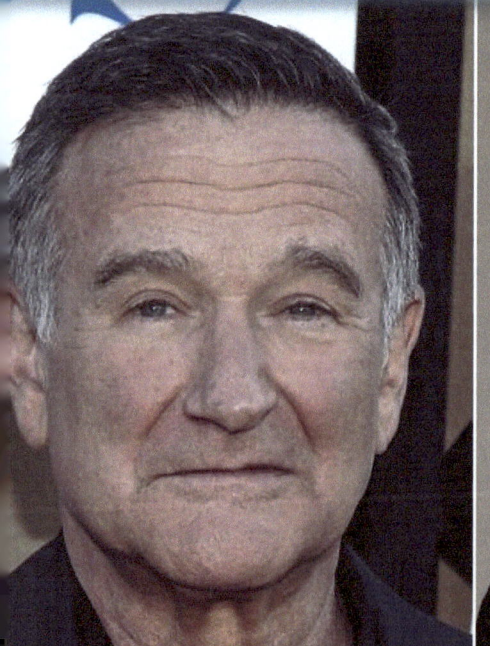

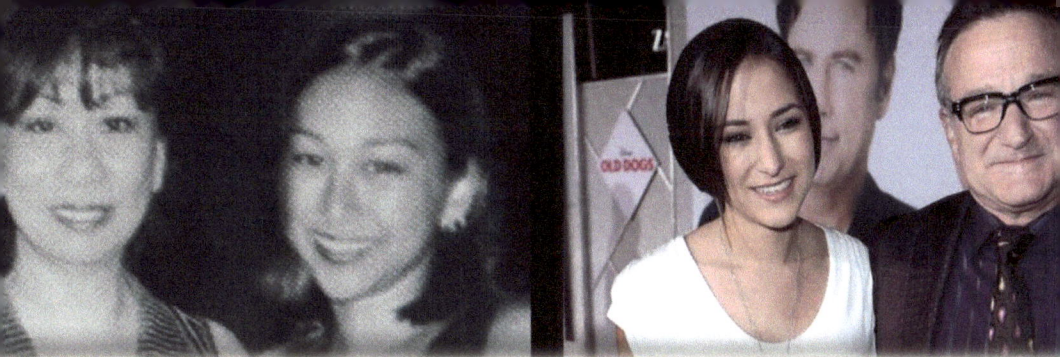

Although I have not been able to explain the connection. I am able to say with almost certainty, (and I am careful) the connection was the most valuable secret any group of individuals could share. It was a secret that was kept from my awareness deliberately. My investigative research led me to find information suggesting child exploitation. I have also interviewed victims who have shed light on the under ground human trafficking cartel, which I briefly touched on in my first book. According to the information, there is a high probability Cecy Groom acted as a liaison Robin Williams used for criminal purposes. It was genius because the number of aliases alone made any attempt at contact-tracing virtually impossible. I suspected Robin Williams and Cindy McCain shared family bloodlines, although I have not made an effort to establish that suspicion as fact. With that said, based on my research it is suggested that Cindy McCain shares family bloodlines with Hilary Clinton and Lady Evelyn De Rothschild. If Robin Williams were part of that same family tree, that would explain his alias "R. William Rheineschild."

Cindy McCain is arguably the most outspoken advocate against human

ALEJANDRO

trafficking and child exploitation, in the State of Arizona. My psychological training tells me that Cindy's philanthropic contributions against child exploitation are too advantageous, and there is too much financial incentive for Cindy's true motive to be honest. But, I am not looking at this from an outside perspective because I have met Cindy personally. My perspective is an inside one. I know first hand how much money she moves in and out of this country; too much not to be questioned. From my understanding, Cindy McCain's criminal network's profits somewhere around three billion dollars annually. I hope to god Cindy McCain files a lawsuit against me, for something.

Her crime ring is responsible for making me homeless, and I have a counter suit bigger than all of her offshore bank accounts put together, ready and waiting. I doubt anything will happen, besides, her statutes of limitations expired in August 2013. Secretly, I would love the opportunity to walk into the Beverly Hills courthouse looking as if I just walked off of skid row, which is something her daughter Meghan knows all about. When Meghan McCain tried to make me believe she were a homeless single mother, I dropped her ass off, (I mean that with love) at the Los Angeles Mission Woman's Shelter. I had no intention of leaving her. I just wanted to see what she would do—it scared her so bad she vomited. It was priceless and

totally worth the $400 traffic ticket I got after I made a wrong turn onto a one-way street and ended up face-to-face with an LAPD traffic cop. The scene was like an exodus out of Liberia (I also mean that with love) and I nearly had to drive onto the sidewalk in order to avoid running someone over. I have to say that I do not know anyone else who has had this much fun with their enemies.

A L E J A N D R O

When I met Cindy McCain in Newport Beach, California nearly four years ago, the name she used was "Cathy Kutzner." Over the years, I have observed how she follows a pattern of picking Jewish surnames as aliases. She then pairs the name with given names beginning with either "C" or "K" such as "Karen" Kathy" "Cathleen" "Catherine" "Cindy" and so forth. Cindy McCain is the genius behind Brookstone Law.

> Brookstone Law Complaints & Reviews - Scam!!!
>
> Brookstone Law Contacts & Informations
>
> ## Brookstone Law
> Posted 2011-02-26 by PLease Help911
>
> ### Scam!!!
> Complaint Rating
>
> Its all the same thing. Damian Kutzner started United Law Group about two years ago with his puppet attorney Sean Rutledge. Damian Kutzner has a 6 million dollar judgment against him from the FTC (http://www.ftc.gov/opa/2009/07/globalmgt.shtm) so his name legally can not be on any business. After United Law Group was raided by the FBI for not servicing clients Damian filed for Bankruptcy and evacuated the building. He was then caught stealing from the building he was forced to leave. Damian is now running another puppet attorney who used to work for United Law Group Vito Torchia Jr! You would think he would be smarter than to see what happened to Sean Rutledge and Robert Buscho and Christian M Dillon. But as its happened for thousands of years history does repeat itself.

She is also the reason the Federal Bureau of Investigation refuses to acknowledge the alleged fraud being committed by Brookstone attorneys; Vito Torchia, Jr. owns Brookstone Law. I know Vito Torchia by the name Samuel Paul Bain Some of his victims know him as "Kevin Wright" of America's Help Center. The Federal Trade Commission was paid $10 million to have Mr. Bain's federal charges for mortgage fraud dropped. Interestingly enough, rap artist Snoop Dogg is one of Cindy McCain's business partners. Senator John McCain and his wife Cindy, also happen to be the original copyright claimants for the song "Alejandro" which was filed under the aliases "Benjamin and Cindy Spigle." (Notice 'Spigle' is misspelled on purpose).

A L E J A N D R O

Coincidentally, John and Karen King use an address belonging to the Goss estate. I would never have been able to connect John and Karen King, to Cindy McCain if Karen King and Cathy Kutzner had not used the same address in Newport Beach, California belonging to Damien Kutzner. Based on the evidence, it seems as if fraud is Cindy McCain's forte; alleged, of course. When the alias name Karen Laterza, showed up on the postal records for 847 Hammond Street, in West Hollywood, I knew Cindy McCain was connected. The fact that Ms. Laterza's company, Health4Life.net, was based in Seattle, Washington only confirmed it. My investigation linked the owner of the domain, to one of Cindy's illegal corporations. Some one leased office space for that same company using my legal name in Santa Ana, California. If they had not, I would not have had the information required to make the association. The reason I waited until now to make this information public was because I have spent the last couple years exhausting myself by pleading to authorities for an investigation. I may be naive, but I am not stupid. I only appeared delusional whenever I made an attempt to communicate this information, without having a complete awareness of how this criminal network was organized. Therefore, I wanted to obtain a more proficient understanding of how the entire puzzle came together first, before making an attempt to discuss it publicly.

Web   Images   News   Videos   Shopping   More ▼   Search tools

About 8,170,000 results (0.56 seconds)

Images for cindy mccain alejandro   Report images

More images for **cindy mccain alejandro**

Alejandro C. Estrada's Blog - Cindy McCain: A Conspiracy ...
www.goodreads.com/.../6409189-cindy-mccain-a-conspiracy-... ▼ Goodreads ▼
Jun 4, 2014 - **Cindy McCain**: A Conspiracy to Commit Murder, Fraud, and Domestic
Terrorism ... View more on **Alejandro** C. Estrada's website ». • flag.

Cindy McCain: Conspiracy to Commit Murder - SlideShare
www.slideshare.net/EstradaAlexC/**cindy-mccain**-conspiracy-to-commit-... ▼
Jun 4, 2014 - Images of corruption involving Lady Gaga, **Alejandro**, the Associated
Press, President Barak Obama, Jay Carney, **Cindy McCain**, mortgage ...

Cindy McCain: Conspiracy to Commit Murder - Slideee.com
www.slideee.com/slide/**cindy-mccain**-conspiracy-to-commit-murder ▼
Jun 4, 2014 - Images of corruption involving Lady Gaga, **Alejandro**, the Associated
Press, President Barak Obama, Jay Carney, **Cindy McCain**, mortgage ...

Whistleblower needs Help by Alex Estrada - GoFundMe
www.gofundme.com/Whistleblower ▼
Jun 11, 2014 - **Cindy McCain's** business has annual profits around $3 Billion dollars.
The majority of her profits come from illegal criminal activity including real ...

Alejandro Estrada | Facebook
https://www.facebook.com/official.**alejandro**.estrada?fref=nf ▼
Alejandro Estrada. 9 likes. Author ... Sherman MD". Listen to Robin William as "
Michael Sherman MD" by **Alex** Estrada 27 ... True Colors — with **Cindy McCain**.

Alex Estrada | LinkedIn
www.linkedin.com/in/**alejandro**ce ▼
West Hollywood, California - Principle at ACE Consulting

Not to mention, talking about these dead ended connectors just sounds like a lot of hearsay and disorganized facts. Especially to someone that my not be part of the organizational structure.

Truth is the most valuable commodity that exists which money cannot buy. Truth is so precious; it is priceless and so rare that few people can recognize it. The more corrupt society becomes; the more dangerous truth is to possess and in the most corrupt societies, communicating it an Act of Defiance equal to treason and domestic terrorism. When truth becomes the enemy, a revolution is unavoidable because the real enemies of the State are those hiding behind the powers of that State. There is no benefit to me by making this information public, and only criminals who have acted against the people of the United States of America have a reason to discredit it. Fortunately, truth is indefensible and clamor is an admission of guilt.

I am not here to debate or discuss. I am here to provide answers, so allow me to reiterate the fact that I am not a theorist. My knowledge comes from first-hand experience and eye witness. My words will be brief because pictures say more than my fingers will ever be able to communicate, and my opposition has done most of that work for me. My job now is to piece it together so that the world may awaken itself and see it for what it is: a billion-dollar farce worth more money than there are gold reserves available on this planet. Moreover, my information is provided free for anyone that makes the effort to find it.

With G-D as my witness: every person, and entity, who has denied me justice, or refused to help me when I have asked to be helped; and/or ridiculed me, excluded me, belittled me, humiliated me, slandered me, and/or attacked me directly or indirectly will be counted among my enemies. My enemies are G-D's enemies and anyone standing against me, stands in vain.

I, Alejandro Carbajal Estrada, am a descendant of David and the Bright Morning Star; I am the Bearer of Light and Bringer of Truth.

REJECT ME ONCE, AND I WILL NEVER ACCEPT YOU.

Those who hate me, hate themselves, and their self-hatred will become the liquefaction of their entire lineage. The debt owed to me for these crimes will remain unsettled, until those who are guilty become eradicated from the face of this earth. Not one second before their entire existence becomes extinct from the human race, will that debt be settled. If the human race needs to be exterminated, in its entirety for that to become a reality, then, by G-D, so be it. Should no authority or agency exist, willing to acknowledge these crimes by bringing those responsible to justice and giving me the recourse owed. Then I pray to G-D to be avenged once and for all.

Considering the fact that my perpetrators hold leadership roles within the Federal government, these crimes qualify as Treason against the Republic of the United States of America and according to the Law, Treason is punishable by death.

Anyone that refuses to respect the authority of Law, is also guilty of Treason.   Therefore my request for justice is completely humble and well within reason.   However, if justice is too much to ask for and

> 1. MY PROPERTY IS NOT RETURNED TO ME.
> 2. I AM UNABLE TO HONOR MICHAEL GOSS'S DYING WISH, AS HIS RIGHTFUL HEIR.

Then may G-D's wrath of pestilence sweep this planet unmercifully until the human DNA is cleansed from every trace of pollution.

Alice's Hungry Hole
and other Savage Beasts

BEHIND EVERY GREAT MAN IS A WOMAN WITH BLOOD ON HER HANDS

aCe Consulting

isabella medical clinic

Osho

Baby, My Whole Work Is to Confuse You!

The day was beautiful. Sunny. Warm. Traffic was light as I progressed towards the freeway entrance on my way to the Los Angeles Superior Courthouse to file some documents against my lawyer's instruction. His name was Todd Stevenson. His office was in the city of Van Nuys, approximately forty miles away, and the referral came from the Los Angeles County Bar Association. The system uses demographics to match potential clients, with lawyers in the immediate geographic location.

At the time, I could not understand how the system matched me up with an attorney so far away. But his interest was high, his energy was upbeat and his motivation seemed confident. He was also the only lawyer willing to talk to me.

I was mentally multitasking and brainstorming ideas when I passed a familiar gated community, and a light bulb suddenly came on. I made a U-turn and decided to delay my trip downtown.

My former client, Cecy Groom, lived in that gated community. Certified Public Accountant by day, Madame 24/7 and politician by night. If I called her filthy, she might have grounds to sue me for libel. As if legal consequences ever stopped me from exposing the truth before; besides, truth does not justify legal action.

My earliest memory of Cecy Groom is a gray image of a hazy room, and the words "*Poot eet en the oeuvin.*"

Stop laughing, that wasn't a joke it was *"Put it in the oven"* in my best attempt to replicate Cecy's mysterious accent; strange because it almost sounds fake. She claims to be from the Philippines; however the Filipino community does not seem to trust her. Probably because she speaks Tagalog with a foreign accent. According to her story, the village she grew up in, has their own distinct dialect, except among the Filipinos I have talked with, no one seems to know the exact location of that village.

I still had the gate code programmed in my car memory, so I drove inside and parked. She was home, and it was show time.

A couple hours later, mad puppy dog eyes, and even some tears I pulled Michael's death certificate out of my briefcase. Cecy eagerly snatched it and began to examine it.

She began to "Oooooh" and "Ahhhh" and then she said, "I see, yep, yep, very interesting," as her eyes scanned the document. Then she asked, "Did you see the body?"

I replied helplessly "No," while shaking my head and lowering my eyes.

"Was there a funeral?" she asked, causing me to get emotional and slightly hysterical. She calmed me down by saying "I'll help you. You need to talk to Jim Burke at City Hall immediately." And she promised to arrange a meeting. Then, she repeated "Michael Goss" under her breath and continued

"This Michael Goss name sounds familiar, who was he? A Doctor?"

"No, a porn director," I answered.

"Porn?"

"Yes, his film studio produced pornography."

"Hmm, I've heard that name somewhere, " Cecy muttered. "Maybe from Michael [Sherman], he'll be here for dinner with a couple other doctors. They're opening a new clinic and I'm supervising them. You'll get to meet the two exchange students from Thailand too."

"Thailand?" I asked, "Which school?"

"I don't know." She answered. "Some place in Orange County."

It seemed odd. Then again, everything seemed off. I blamed my perception on my post-traumatic syndrome.

Jim Burke held the title of Director of Public Safety for the City of Cerritos. Cecy had arranged an 8PM meeting at City Hall. She informed me he was one of her "links" and that his connections with the Sheriff's Department would help me. However, when I arrived, the deputy on watch told me Mr. Burke was on vacation. This seems to be contagious because so was the detective at the Palm Springs Police Department whenever I tried to contact him regarding the break-in at the house on Broadmoor; and the LAPD detective left on vacation the same day he had scheduled a meeting with me concerning the house in Hollywood that burned to the ground.

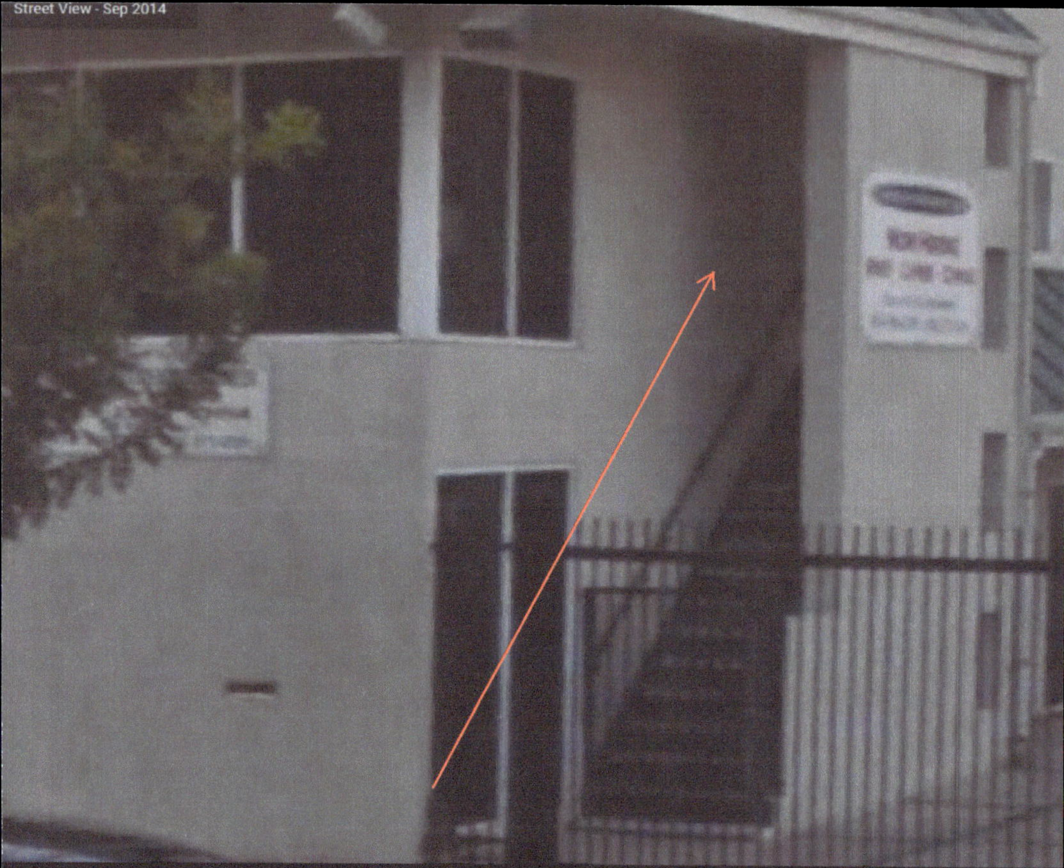

I kept telling myself these were all coincidental, and I began to think I was developing some paranoia. As for the building in the above image, allow me to explain: Cecy asked me to come work for her again and like an idiot I agreed. One of her clients was a medical personnel firm. The office building looked more like a private home than a medical company. If you notice, there are two different structures. They are connected and share an adjoining wall. The two levels of the front building are visible and apparent. The levels of the back building are equivocal; there can be two levels, or possibly three. When taking a closer look, one is able to detect least three levels and perhaps a basement or semi

A L E J A N D R O

subterranean level. Notice the long thin window that faces the street. In front of that window are stairs that lead to a landing and from that landing the stairs continue. At the top is the entrance to the accounting department. There are a series of master bedroom suites and a full kitchen on the first floor of the front building. Sort of like a motel, except with sliding glass doors instead of conventional doors; each unit faces the parking lot. I was not allowed in that part of the building, and I cannot recall if there was a connecting stairway inside because I had to use the exterior stairway to get to the second floor. The top floor had office spaces and storage.

ALEJANDRO

Then there was that mysterious middle floor of the back building that no one talked about. The place gave me the creeps. It still does, and I swore I heard people having sex throughout the building. I thought I was losing my mind which was contributing to the effects on my PTSD. So instead of waiting for Cecy inside the building, I would walk down the street to the French bakery.

Then one day, the entire place was buzzing with activity. According to their story, it was some kind of "job fair." They were "hiring" and conducting "interviews." I don't ask questions. Except, I ran into someone I knew, downstairs in the kitchen, and I realized they were filming pornography. The fact that it was a secret makes me believe it was illegal pornography.

That day instead of having coffee at the French bakery, I decided to confront the issue publicly. As I walked into the accounting office, I said very casually, "There sure is a lot of sex business going on " and the entire room went dumbfounded.

"What do you mean?" Cecy asked

"I mean, the *'Fuck me harder'* sounds... *'Give me that cock.'* You know the sound of hookers choking on dick. *That's what I mean*."

One of the employees answered "Yeah, I heard it earlier."

I interjected "Apparently; they film pornography here. I ran into someone

I used to work with, in the porn business, downstairs."

Suddenly it was time for Cecy and I to leave. I was not allowed back after that, and if Cecy wanted to play games, I was determined to give her one hell of a ride. I later confirmed the owner of that company, Ann Kushy, was indirectly involved with the porn industry. If I understood correctly, she scouts filming locations. That confirmation did not help my PTSD; it made it worse. Nonetheless, I tried to brush it off and convinced myself the problem was in my head. But, my head was not a problem.

Long Pork

My days with Cecy consisted of client meetings, long lunches and even longer dinners. One afternoon Cecy tried handing me a plastic bag filled with meat and asked,

"Do you know what to do with that?"

I refused to touch it and said "No, I order food, not make it" which sparked some tense laughter.

I had no idea where she could have bought the mystery meat. I was

ALEJANDRO

with Cecy the entire day. That day we visited three medical clinics and even skipped lunch. I had no idea how she managed to pull that rabbit out of her ass and under my nose.

I noticed how the cuts of meat were oddly shaped. None of the pieces matched. They did not resemble any butcher's cut I had seen before. The butcher's paper was brown like a brown paper shopping bag. The flesh was light red, almost pink, and it gave me a strange feeling that to this day, I am unable to explain.

She said to me " I think we should *'poot eet een the ouvin'*"

"Poot eet een the ouvin" triggered my subconscious and I remembered something that had been deeply repressed. Those memories from my childhood suddenly resurfaced. The hazy room became crisp and clear. I remembered that I would pretend to sleep during nap time. The reason the room appeared hazy was because I was squinting my eyes to give the impression I was asleep. At the time, I did not understand what I was witnessing, but now as an adult, it makes sense.

My earliest memories from that preschool during nap time, are of watching Cecy Groom as she molested some of the other boys. For years, I told myself those memories were not real, but today the haunting reality is hard to ignore.

My focus returned to the present time by the smell of the meat which was a peculiar and unfamiliar odor that gave off a sweet and pungent stench that made me sick to my stomach. There was something about it I just did not trust. That night at dinner, I gave my serving to Michael Sherman [Robin Williams].

"This meat is the best I've ever tasted Cecy!" Michael [Aquino] Sherman kept repeating in between mouthfuls. I noticed how Michael looked different that night then how I remembered him, but again I blamed it on my trauma and dismissed the discrepancy.

This was around the same time I started noticing very subtle differences in Michael that did not make sense to me. The way he felt changed. How do I explain that?

Michael and I had always had an intimate connection. He is a dangerous man, except I always found comfort in him. He gave me a sense of security and that caused me to lower my guard.

However, then there were times when Michael felt like a stranger. The feeling of safety would be absent, and the energy was almost abrasive, as if he were a different person, like a Jekyll and Hyde. Sometimes, when I referenced things in the past, he acted completely disheveled as if I was lying to him.

But I told myself that everyone has off-days. I am moody so that must have been the explanation. I told myself that Michael Sherman was just unpredictable, and that must have been our common ground.

I have learned to stop making excuses for the world around me. Life is fucked up, and so are the people.

That night after everyone had left Cecy whispered to me,

"Michael Sherman knows what happened to your friend. Ask him."

Those words became the motivating factor behind my decision to ask Michael Sherman[1] for help; her advice led me to believe Michael was the

---

1 To clarify, I try and place either [RW] (Robin Williams) or [Aquino] after the name <ichael Sherman or after Michael and before Sherman, in order to differntiate which individual I believe was playing the role of Michael Sherman at that time, since both were playing the role of "Michael Sherman." The evidence I found of Cecy Groom with Robin's daughter Zelda Williams, confirmed this.   Based on my personal experience, and my training as a psychologist, I have adapted my interpersonal communication skills in order to compensate for deception. No one enjoys being caught doing something bad. In addition, our social culture places a negative stigma on lying which in turn has the potential to create a volatile situation. Therefore, confronting deception is not only counterproductive, but also dangerous. Doing so

only person that could help me. What I did not understand was the reason he would never help me.

---

may potentially endanger the life of the victim or target of the trickery. When someone is caught lying that becomes a behavioral pattern, and it would be irresponsible and negligent to assume the individual is trustworthy. The fact is, one lie equals many lies, and we must assume everything that the person says, will be untrue, or a variation of the truth.

The Confrontation

My involvement with Cecy Groom did not last much longer from that point. It was like a volcanic eruption that no witness will easily forget. It took three days, from start to finish before the relentless fire storm burned itself out.

Reevaluating the situation now, I understand how those chain of events led to such a diabolical dissolution. The amount of hateful, childish and petty games Michael Goss subjected me to prior to his death, was so painfully traumatic, it may have fractured my psyche. When I found myself repeating the same behavior with Cecy, it drove me to the point of insanity that only mortal violence was going to resolve. I arrived at Cecy's house around 3pm. Cecy had an evening engagement in Los Angeles, and we decided to take the morning off. Except, when I showed up, she was not there. Cecy lives in an affluent community. The neighbors are high-level professionals.

During the day, the neighborhood was usually deserted. However, this day someone was having a party and every parking space was taken. I searched for a place to park without luck. I drove down the last street in the development, and I noticed the computer guy had parked his car along the curve of the cul-de-sac. It appeared, to me, as if his intention was for

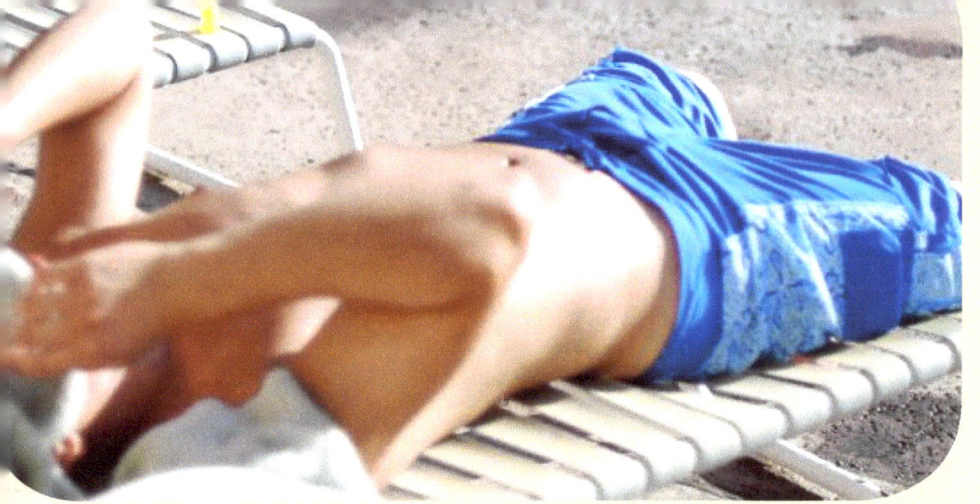

me not to know he were there, and this became the catalyst that set the first domino falling. I ended up double parking in front of a fire hydrant, and fuck the fire because I was about to lose it.

I rang the doorbell, and heard footsteps shuffling upstairs; then I saw someone looking through one of the windows. I rang it again. Ten times, then my kettle began to whistle, so to speak. I held down the buzzer for at least ten minutes, each second compounding the pressure of the steam building inside my temper until it exploded. I began circling the house like a hungry wolf starving himself crazy. Then I tried the back door. Cecy always kept it open, for that horny little cat. But it was locked. I immediately picked up one of the metal patio chairs, as if it were a reflex, and had to stop myself from throwing it through the sliding glass door. That was when the prissy little bitch called me, and made the worst mistake of that entire day. He lied to me as if I were a mentally retarded, blind Chernobyl victim.

He said, "I'm not there; I went--"

ALEJANDRO

ALEJANDRO

And I cut him off like a barracuda, " Bullshit motherfucker! How the fuck do you expect to get your lying, worthless ass, back into the fucking house with the god damned, fucking, shit door locked? You genius fuck!"

Then he hung up on me, and it was apparent he had some death wish. The main circuit breaker is on the side of the garage located inside of a maintenance shed.   It has no lock.   So, like a character in a Stephan King novel, I pulled it.   Once the power was cut off, I raised the garage door manually.   My Adrenaline was skyrocketing; my heart was in my throat, and I was going to kill this son of a bitch for treating me like a castrato Quasi Modo. I remembered one of Michael's assault rifles was still in my car.   Lord knows I was about to walk into some deranged Felini meets Pompeii rendition of Sodom and Gamora.   One thing I knew, he was not alone and I needed insurance.   As I walked to my car, my brain raced trying to figure out how I was going to pull off "self-defense" to the cops. Thankfully, I was able to calm myself and decided to call Cecy instead,

I yelled "What the fuck is going on inside that house Cecy?" so loud that my voice bounced off every house on her street.

She was cautious, too cautious, " Alex, calm down. What do you mean?" and I knew by her tone, she was fully aware of what was taking place.

I answered, "I mean that son of a bitch employee of yours is getting double fucked inside your house and charging you for it." Then I hung up and removed myself from the situation.

The most insulting was the blow to my ego. The rejection was unbearable, and my reaction gave it away. In fact, the trauma I have suffered from this type of degrading humiliation has destroyed my self-esteem, self-image, and self-confidence. Sex was my area of expertise. There was nothing else I had a better mastery of than sex. Sex was a form of communication I used in every aspect of my life. It was more casual than a dinner engagement and more efficient than words. The people in my world went out of their way to get my attention, and I had grown to expect this from the people around me. Except now I was being treated like a leper. Less attractive people were calling me ugly, belittling me, insulting me and rejecting me in the most hateful way anyone could have done it. I felt that my humility was a gift for those I allowed to share my company. It was valuable enough for me to market.

Michael Goss paid me a five digit monthly salary just to have me present because my Gift radiated and filled every room in every one of our homes. Michael Goss soon learned that when I was unhappy, that Gift was equally as painful as it was pleasant, when I was happy. Cecy Groom was about to face another facet of that Gift, because it becomes Hell Fire when I am angry.

I sent Cecy images of me when I was in grammar school. It was obvious they made her uncomfortable. She could not look at them longer than a couple seconds. I came at her like a tiger; hunting her with a stealthy eloquence until I pinned her to a corner of the room. Then, with a full but calm voice, I asked her, "Who the fuck am I, Cecy? And she snapped like a green bean. I was caught completely off guard when she met my crazy, and raised it to a whole new level of insanity. She became violent, punching me with both fists while screaming profanities and thrashing her head from side to side like Mommy Dearest at midnight.

ALEJANDRO

I swear to god; all she needed was a can of Comet, and it would have been epic. That incident took place nearly five years ago. I have not seen her since and have no wish to see her again. More importantly, she remembered me.

The Wizard and the Emerald City

A true story about a Monkey, a Circus Freak, and a Blind Magician

It was love at first sight.

He said, "Hey Alex," proudly, in a boasting tone, then paused briefly to pat himself on the back, and continued "isn't it Gardner Day?"

The mere sight of this son of a bitch made my blood boil, and I snapped back " --It sure is, Wetback, aren't you late for work?"

I did not skip a beat. The entire room went quiet, and I knew that whoever he was, he had to have been someone important. Almost a decade later I found out just how high up the social ladder he was, and if someone had told me then, I would not have believed it.

The name he gave me was 'Grant' and a reverse lookup produced the name 'Grant Covell" an IBM consultant based in Minnesota who worked in Boston and Chicago with the company Katz Media. Except according to Grant, he was a real estate developer. It gets better because the Grant Covell in Boston is supposed to be of Asian decent. The best part was how the Vice President of Public Relations, at Katz Media, was "Michael Sherman."

I told myself it had to be a coincidence and decided to run a background check for "Michael Sherman" in New York City. The results gave me the same birthday and social security number as the Michael Sherman I knew in Beverly Hills. (I have learned that coincidence does not exist.)

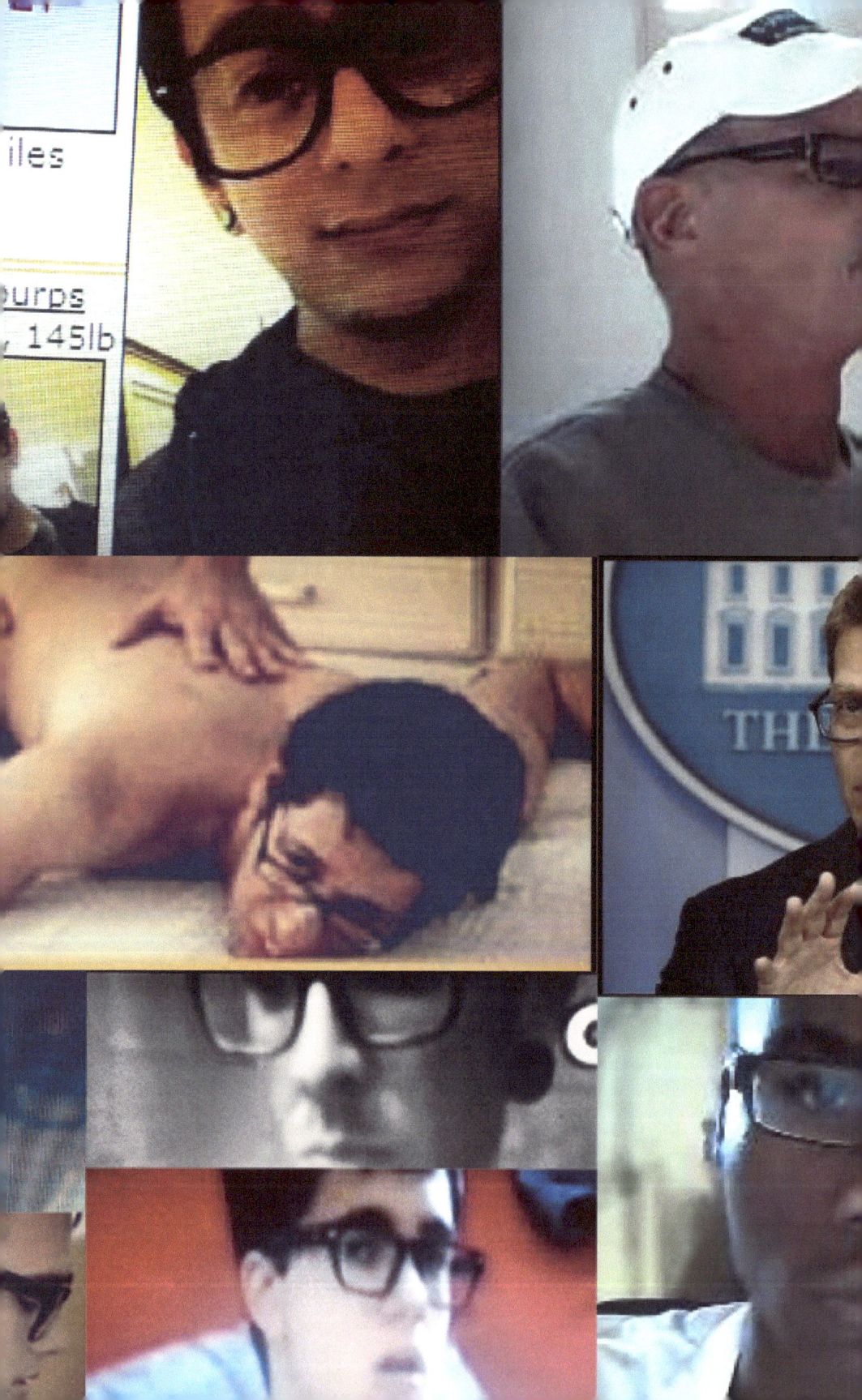

Then I caught "Grant Covell" with Michael [Aquino] Sherman in Phoenix, Arizona over a long weekend, entertaining a handful of prostitutes while at an military base. To say the shit hit the fan, would be an understatement.

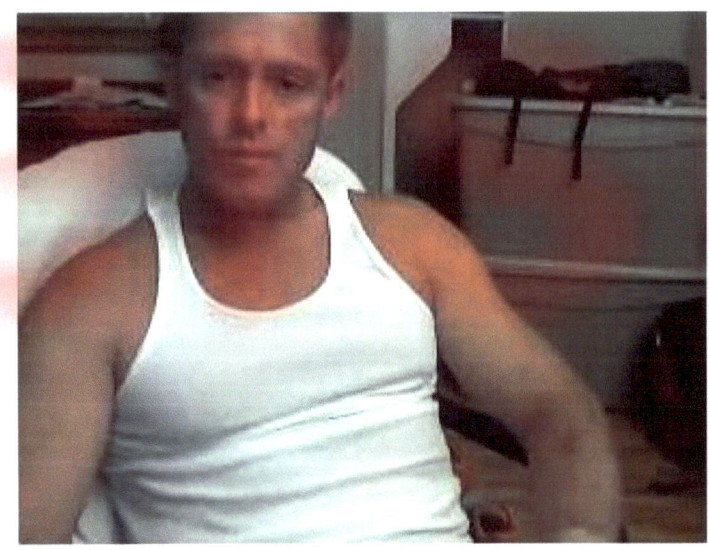

But let me back up, I'm going too fast. Let's try that again, slower this time. Michael Sherman and I had been at the office late on a Friday. He may have briefly mentioned an impromptu trip to Phoenix, although I do not recall him bringing it up. I left the office shortly after midnight and on my drive home, I had this feeling he was going out of town. I immediately dismissed the thought. Michael Sherman [RW] did not fly commercially, and it is almost impossible to get the clearance out of Orange County airport past curfew.

Clearly, I thought, he would have said something. Well, the following day, when Michael Sherman failed to show up for an afternoon meeting, my suspicion was confirmed. Maybe paranoia would be more accurate, Whatever the case, I sort of lost it.

I had been studying the behavioral patterns of both "Grant" and "Michael" for nearly two years, convinced there was a connection. Now was my chance to test out my theory and establish fact from fiction so, on Sunday afternoon I approached "Grant" and preempted him by saying playfully,

"Hey Grant, according to Michael Sherman you boys had a blast in Phoenix"

To which he replied slowly,

"It was *guuuuuuuud*. Wow you sure know a lot."

Moments later Michael Sherman called to apologize.

He informed me how some "government action" came up. According to his story, a trip to Phoenix was urgent and "top-secret." I don't think he realized I spent the last day and a half watching him fist-fuck the grand canyon of hookers via web cam. Well, how could he, I logged in under stealth. I always log in under the radar whenever I plan to record something.

Michael Sherman went on about how he was at an unspecified air force base, and the entire thing reeked of bullshit. So much, that the very thought of researching air force bases in Arizona still, to this day, makes me sick to my stomach. I just listened. Almost mutely, as he groveled. He went on and on. About how he wanted me to come along. Then he immediately backtracked, with excuses. He said I needed to have clearance to be on base. If I were there, I would have to wait at the hotel while he was busy on the base and his attempt made things worse. After all, this took place over Columbus Day weekend. Most of the guys at the base were out on holiday leave. I will die and never find out what exactly happened that weekend, and that is ok because I have a point of reference to know all too well what may have occurred. It was evident to me someone got initiated, and that always involves a human toilet reenactment. Scatty Cathy, I may have said too much, but all those lovely images flooding my imagination was enough to bring me back to my senses, and I dropped the argument. Things went back to normal. At least what I considered to be normal.

Then a couple months later my image showed up on an adult pay per view website in an advertising campaign entitled "The Predator and the Prey."

That truly was the piece de la résistance.

Someone Photoshop'ed my face onto the body of someone being sexually penetrated by an older man. A married older man because he's wearing a wedding ring. I was fucked. Raped publicly and emasculated in front of the world audience. Wait. Not just a global audience, but on a social networking website as well. I decided to confront Grant Covell indirectly, not to accuse him of anything, but to vent out my frustration.

A L E J A N D R O

I was testing him because according to my research, Grant Covell was farming out IT projects from under IBM's nose. One of the projects he managed was for an adult pay-per-view website. I was able to locate the mass e-mail Grant sent to his underground network of consultants. My instinct was telling me; Grant's professional network was responsible for attacking me, and as I anticipated, Grant Covell took the bait.

Immediately following my conversation with Grant Covell, the web servers were deliberately taken down for approximately four hours, and when they came back Online, every illegally obtained image of me was gone.

The problem for Grant was that I did not make any demands or requests.

All I did was forward him a copy of the image and a statement to the effect of "This is the kind of shit I've been living with since those assholes killed Michael."

After a short exchange, he panicked and offered me a cash settlement if I would sign a non-disclosure agreement regarding the incident. I agreed, but he breached our contract.

During a previous conversation, Grant informed me he knew the well-known civil rights attorney, Gloria Allred, personally. By this point I knew " Grant Covell" was just an alias. So, I decided to contact the law firm of Allred, Maroko, and Goldberg here in Los Angeles, regarding Grant's breach of contract. I was hoping they might be able to provide me with Grant's real identity. The case information I provided claimed my civil rights were being violated by the LAPD, LASD and the Bureau of Investigation for the agency's effort to cover-up Michael Goss's murder.

I claimed the illegal use of my image and misappropriation of my likeness were examples of the retaliation tactics used to target and demoralize me as a victim.

I deliberately omitted a contact name on Grant's phone record and only provided the phone number because I wanted the law firm to do the research. I knew they would not get far before hitting a dead-end.

I expected that the phone records would make its way in front of Ms. Allred after the firm would be unable to get a positive identity of the owner of that phone number. Surely, Ms. Allred would recognize Grant's number. They were close personal friends according to Grant. Depending on the type of relationship Mr. Covell and Ms. Allred shared, then it was possible that Allred, Maroko, and Goldberg might have a conflict of interest in pursuing the case.

Ultimately, I expected this law firm would act with a high value of ethics by disclosing Grant's real identity. If such a conflict existed, the reason would be connected to his celebrity or the celebrity of his position. It was obvious from this point he worked in government, and I was under the naivety that the government should be held accountable for maintaining complete transparency.

Ms. Somers, an attorney at the firm, contacted me. According to Ms. Somers, Grant Covell had not been authorized to offer a settlement. Ms. Somers also went on to inform me Grant did not have the assets to back up his offer. By doing so, Ms. Somers created collusion on behalf of the law firm in order to protect Grant's real identity, and it was evident to me, they had been advised to expect my legal query. I fell into a depression. I began to lose hope. My outlook grew discouraged, and several months later I came across an image of Grant Covell in an important news publication, giving a press conference at the White House.

Although, I soon learned that Jay Carney was not as famous for being the

White House Press Secretary, as he was infamous for being a compulsive liar. The man has a clinical condition that prevents him from being able to say anything that is not an entirely ridiculous absurdity or unfathomable piece of fiction. It is a sad situation. Jay Carney should be admitted to the hospital and placed under the direct care of a physician. For his wellbeing and the wellbeing of society. But instead of addressing this issue responsibly; Mr. Carney's peers use his mental illness as if it were comedy relief and their inaction has jeopardized the wellbeing of the entire nation.

MARGIE SOMERS IS AN ATTORNEY AT THE LAW FIRM ALLRED; MAROKO AND GOLDBERG LOCATED AT 6300 WILSHIRE BLVD., SUITE 1500 IN THE CITY OF LOS ANGELES, CALIFORNIA (90048). I WAS A VICTIM, BUT DESPITE HER LEGAL OBLIGATION, SHE PASSED JUDGMENT ON MY CHARACTER FOR THE CRIMES USED TO VICTIMIZE ME.

My case had grown cold regarding the Goss estate until I found the missing link between Jay Carney, Gloria Allred, Cindy McCain, Robin Williams and Cecy Groom.

I have done the job that the Federal Bureau of Investigation was obligated to do.   The cost of hiring a certified forensic specialist to conduct a forensic investigation and analysis of the evidence costs less than $1000.00.   It is humbling, or humiliating, to know I have spent more money on pairs of shoes because my future is reliant on a forensic analysis.   Once I am able to establish who killed Michael Goss, the rest falls into place.   My attorney, Todd Stevenson, advised me against diminishing the importance of the position Michael Goss appointed me, after I expressed concerns regarding criticism I might face for defending my legal right to Michael's inheritance.   When I met Todd Stevenson, I was emotionally devastated, and I was still in the process of trying to make sense of an illogical situation.   Mr. Stevenson also reminded me how the only thing that mattered, was Michael's decision to make me his beneficiary, not other people's opinion about that decision.   I had a feeling Todd Stevenson was trying to sabotage me, so as a test I told him the insurance documents were inside a safe under the house. They destroyed three large trees and dug up the yard looking for that safe.   In fact, they ripped out the entire floor in the house looking. They violated California State law and City Ordnance doing so, but I got labeled as "delusional."

Apparently, this is what delusion must look like then:

A L E J A N D R O

When they could not find the documents, they forged them and cashed out a life insurance policy worth half a million dollars. Two years after publishing my first book, not only am I still homeless, but now I have been permanently disabled by the damages I have suffered. Cecy Groom would be aware of the damage one forensic analysis would cost her criminal network, and I cannot blame her for acting in self-preservation. However, I will never forgive her decision to invade my once peaceful life, especially considering I had the power to do to her, what she does with her clients. Cecy Groom failed to recognize the genuine honesty of my character because she was blinded by her demons.

Blackmail is for cowards who do not know how to use a bidet correctly. There is no incentive large enough for me to consider committing a crime. Because of circumstance I am a penniless millionaire, but a millionaire none the less. Although, the difference between me and people like Cecy Groom and Cindy McCain, is how I earned it honestly. If it had not been honest, they would not have been able to steal it from me, like a pack of hyenas. This case becomes national interest because in the United States of America; law protects victim's rights. Therefore, the collusion these people created prevented me from taking legal action against them. Their actions become more than just a civil rights violation.

It is treason because this corruption is not limited to local or state level authorities acting based on a social prejudice.

People who knew me on a personal level attacked me and they abused their political power in order to protect their own interests. Therefore, their actions compromised the infrastructure of the nation. Perhaps the most devastating aspect of this entire ordeal, at least for me, may have occurred in August 2014, when actor Robin Williams committed suicide. But if it had not been for that tragedy, I may not have been able to connect Mr. Williams to the man I knew as Michael Sherman and the alias "R. William Rheineschild." On several occasions, I communicated to authorities I suspected Michael Sherman's real identity was R. William Rheineschild. Even though I never believed R. William Rheineschild was the real name, I had no evidence that showed otherwise. So, I made an effort to seek out the people who knew this individual personally, namely Gloria Allred and Jay Carney. Not only did I find answers, but I also found evidence that supported my gut feeling.

According to Michael Sherman, he was homeless. I had no idea homeless people wore Armani suits, but who am I to question someone that is homeless and struggling to survive. If anything, I could relate to Michael Sherman and this commonality may have brought us closer. Ironically, this character role became a security blanket, if you will. Michael Sherman was Robin William's safe place.

Robin Williams

As long as he was Michael Sherman, there was no need to treat me like everyone else who knew he was famous. On one occasion I had his daughter, Zelda Williams, in my custody for approximately 10-12 hours. I have not been able to figure out the reason behind that decision, and the fact that our time together was unsupervised makes the situation more confusing to me. During that visit, she confirmed the real meaning behind the song lyrics for the song "Alejandro." I told Zelda that I did not care what Michael Sherman's real identity was because not knowing may have been the one thing keeping me safe. I felt my life would be endangered if Michael Sherman's real identity became known; she agreed. I had no prerogative in exposing Michael Sherman, if anything; I made an effort to defend Michael Sherman as if it were a real identity. After all, my first book was dedicated to 'Michael Sherman." With that said, I am not so naive. I knew it was not his real name. Although, I honestly believed Michael Sherman would help me, but first I had to earn his trust.

I also believed Michael Sherman when he promised me one of his lawyers would handle my legal case. I had no reason to doubt him; his lawyers were among the dirtiest in the nation. I needed lawyers like that on my team. When that never transpired, I knew there must be bigger money involved on the line. Money big enough to prevent them from fighting like wild dogs over my piece of the pie.

By trusting Michael Sherman's [RW] promise to me, I may have made the worst decision for my future. I realize now that I will suffer from that error in judgment for the rest of my life. My last exchange with Robin Williams, I asked whether he believed I was mentally impaired or just clinically insane. Because, only a blind fool, who were monkey shit nuts, would shove his fist up his ass, and ask his enemies to help him find it. I clarified how this charade was so far past gullible; it was malicious. I spent almost a year living with Michael Sherman (RW). He knew about my sixth sense better than most people.

I then told Michael Sherman [RW], the most disappointing aspect, was how the people in my life believe I am a retarded eunuch. Who doesn't know the difference between a glory hole and a urinal.

I finally told Robin that I only wanted what they owed me. My property, my royalties; and compensated for the damages they caused me. So that I could take the broken pieces of my life, and finally be allowed to grieve. In peace. Because I have to mourn first, before I can move on with my life. As long as strangers occupy my home, I am stuck in this place stagnating. How can I mourn, when Michael Goss still has not had a funeral?

Robin ignored me. So my next message informed him that I wanted to settle out of court and put this behind us. In my e-mail, I specified that if we went to court, my claim of punitive damages would be $100 million. We both knew that figure might double after a court finished auditing every last penny. At that time, I was unaware of his real identity. My focus was on Cindy McCain because she was the original copyright claimant for the song "Alejandro." He finally responded "Correct" and a month later he was found dead at his home in northern California.

Evidently, someone took me serious and whoever that was, they also believed Robin Williams was a liability for allowing me to get as close as I was able to get. Above all the deception and cruel intentions, Robin was still the closest thing I had to an ally. This tragedy was so much more calamitous for me because every significant person in my life always ends up dead. The survivor's guilt is fucked up, to say the least.

When I think back to the time Robin, and I spent, the memories are as sweet as they are bitter. I trusted him with my life. He was a father-figure. Without a shadow of a doubt, Robin saw me as one of his kids.

Without him, I might not still be alive. However, this was a stark contrast to the abrasive moody man Cecy Groom introduced me to. The biggest difference between Michael Sherman and Robin Williams was that Robin showed me affection and Michael never touched me. The affection I received from Robin was wholesome and genuine. I have been touched by enough men, to know the difference between conditional lust and unconditional concern. I feel as if he wanted to help me. For all I know, he might have tried to negotiate some settlement on my behalf. If so, it could have cost him his life.

There was something about the media coverage on Robin Williams that stuck out to me in a unique way. The same way every other significant interlinking connection jumped out at me in an obscure but bold attention catching way. My gut instinct recognized Robin on a personal level. I began researching. Unlike most people, I search images. When I begin a web search, I allow my sixth sense to lead me from one image to the next. This technique has proven to be 100% successful. As I searched, I noticed how some of Robin's images felt familiar, others were not so much. Then there were those images that seemed more than familiar.

There are copies of every email, text message, and voice message, sent by me and received since Michael Goss's death. I also have GPS tracking data for the routes I have taken.

88

From my voice mail in-box, I took two of Robin's most recent voice mails, exported them and then published the data on SoundCloud. Next, I began posting the link on social media. The forensic challenge I faced was that "Michael Sherman's" character role was a Polish medical doctor. Every aspect of this character was plausible. Except one: Dr. Sherman was supposed to have been the former KGB Olympic doctor for the Polish National Team, during the Cold War era. I had no need to research whether or not that person existed.

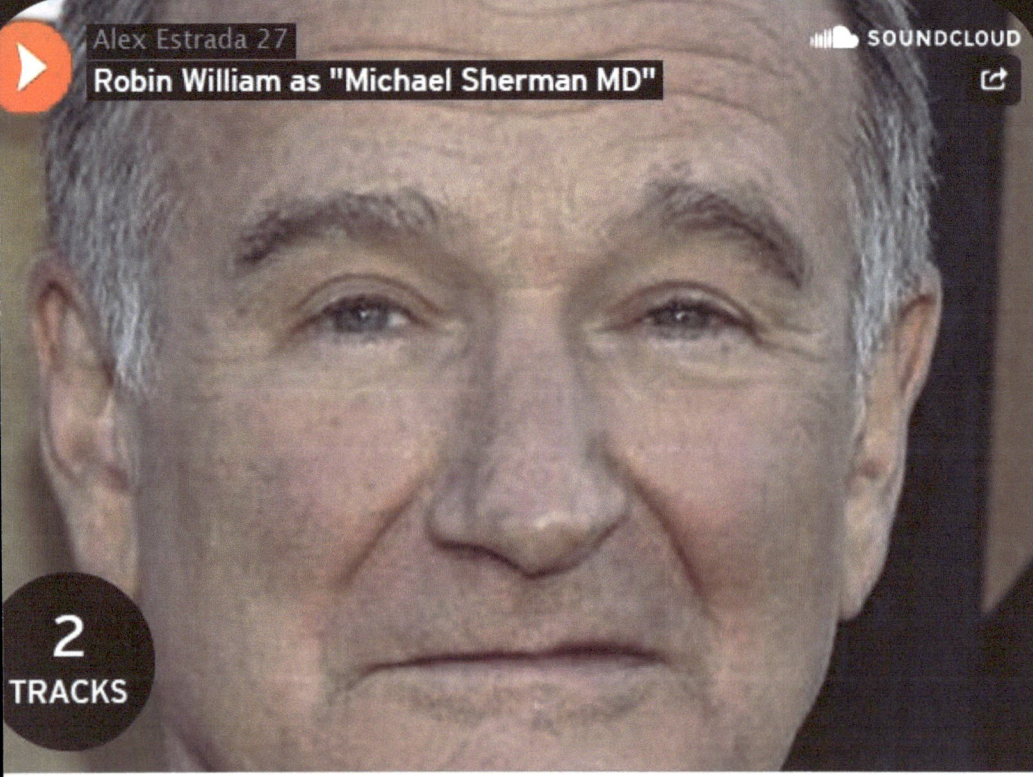

At least the role-playing and Improv was creative. Playing along was effortless, and it was even therapeutic on some level.

"Michael Sherman" was leasing out office space in a commercial building in Santa Ana. California. The lease was paid for six month in advance when the management company evicted us. The best part though was that he was one of the owners.

I was not supposed to know, and I made sure to put him through it every chance I got. None of the various pieces of equipment worked. They were just movie props. I know because I tried plugging in one of the ultrasound machines.

Until now, I had not shared that with anyone. After we had been kicked out, we continued to "squat." Robin was like a mischievous child. It was nice for me to see him having fun. The funniest part was how it was his building. No doubt the partners would still have been just as pissed off if they found out what we were up to.

The same night that the property management company changed the door locks, I drilled them out. It must have been around 3'O'Clock in the morning, and I used an industrial power drill. The building had a courtyard and that night, the entire Santa Ana Civic Center heard me as I drilled out the door locks. The Santa Ana Police Department was half a block away.

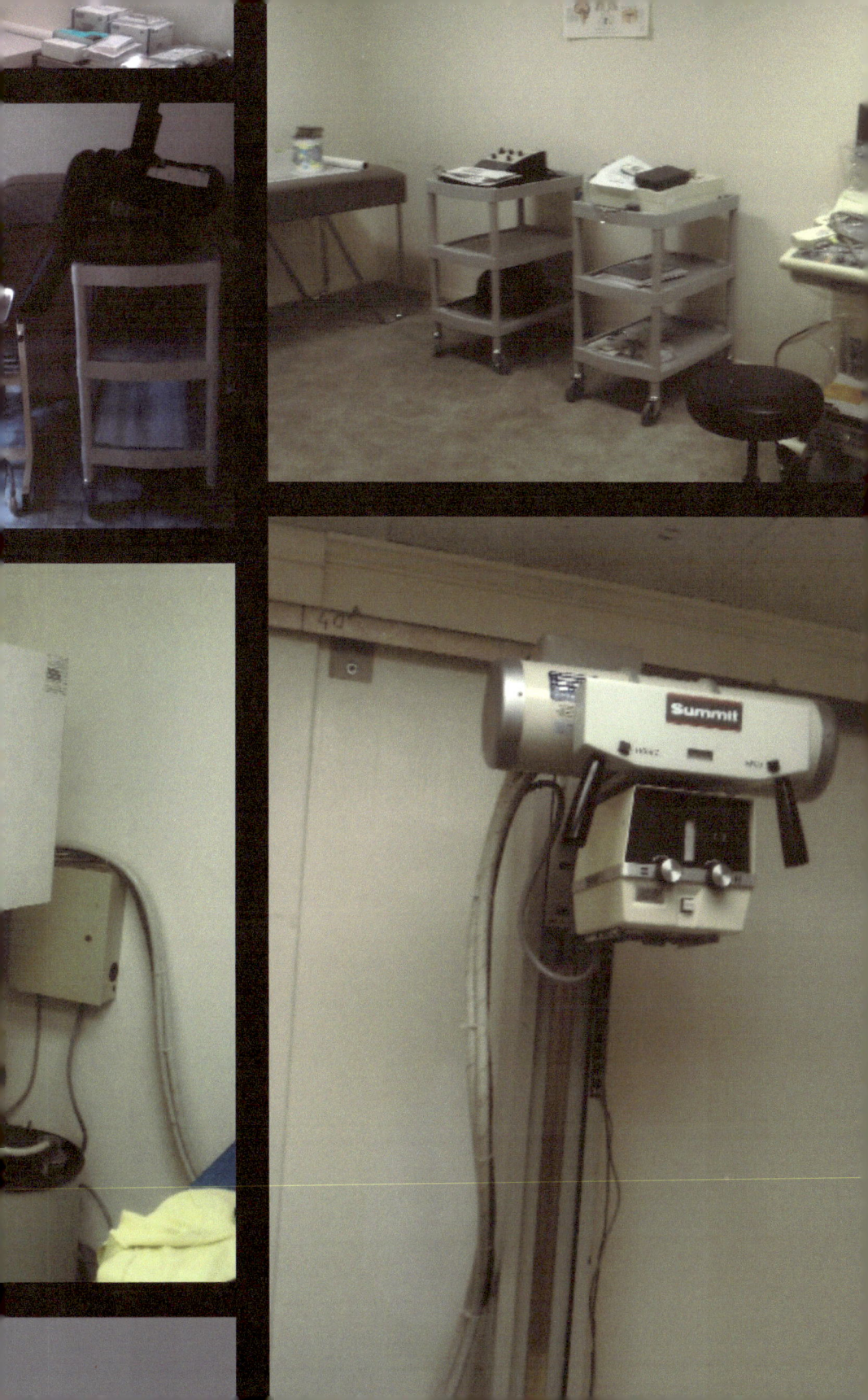

The building had 24 hour camera surveillance, so when not one cop showed up, it was enough confirmation for me to know the rest.

In comparison, the night Paul Bain broke a window the cops were there in less than 5 minutes. The morning I pinned the maid's head between the toilet and wall with her trash cart, the cops were there in less than 5 minutes. Hold on. Not just the cops, but the same cop showed up every time.

The reason I had to put the maid in her place, (I say that with love) was because the path she chose to go down, was heading towards the wrong end point. Someone had to enlighten her. I had no issue being the bad guy because they already hated me. One afternoon, I borrowed the key to the Woman's rest room; from the lady that leased the office next to us. The maid walked in; we had words. Words; I will not repeat. According to one of the trustees, the maid claimed I was masturbating in the woman's rest room, and he knew better. The building had cameras. Although, the cameras were not visible. Apparently, the maid was not aware of their placement. The maid also claimed I was smoking marijuana. It amazes me sometimes, how the little people, often never learn, how the bigger people are always watching them.

So, one morning while the maid was cleaning the men's rest room, I communicated a very clear warning to back. The fuck off, my ass. The problem was; I don't speak Spanish.   I am not sure what I said to her, but whatever it was, it worked.

When I returned to the office, I made a beeline to the very last exam room. As I shuffled past the doctor's office, I said to Michael Sherman [RW] "The cops are coming."

Then, I changed clothes so when the cops did show up, not only was the maid's description of me wrong, but I had no idea what she was talking about. She kept stuttering like someone suffering from a mental illness. Mumbling incoherently about something I planned to do;   I don't know. Whatever it was, it involved her family.   I turned to the officer and said,

"Officer that bitch is crazy. I don't even speak Spanish."

From the point on, she was a church mouse.   Nowhere in sight, and not even the sound of wind against whiskers.   The way God intended.

We had fun, Robin and I.   I wish his children could have known him the way I knew him.   After his death, I forwarded copies of his voice mails to individuals I know, who also knew Robin in person.   I needed to know if the voice on my voice mail belongs, or could have belonged, to Robin Williams. No one has told me no.

I submitted the voice mails to Lt. Boyd at the Marin County Sheriff's Department.   I also provided the evidentiary files I had organized for my lawsuit against Cindy McCain. Lt. Boyd censored every piece of evidence I provided. I expected he would. That is the reason I took the precaution to copyright the voice mails.

I cannot imagine living without a sixth sense. Take away any other sense, and life goes on. The sixth sense, however, is the most important sense human beings possess. It is the one sense, we never lose. The sixth sense might be our strongest sense. But, the majority of people have a misconception that associates it with having a psychic ability. I am not talking about Diane Warwick, when I reference the term 'sixth sense'. When I use the term 'sixth sense' I am speaking about that instinct human beings have that allows us to feel color and taste it. It is the instinct we have that tells us which traffic lane another driver will change to, regardless if that driver uses an indicator. The instinct that tells us when danger is near. In a room without lights, it is the one sense that knows where to find the light switch.

As a society, we associate it with crazy. We are conditioned to think this way. When people react physically to the intangible, our social conditioning is reinforced because the display appears to be crazy. To clarify, I am not talking about little boys that see dead people. That only happens in films and things that happen in movies, should be kept in movies. Movies are not real life. As common sense as that may sound, a large part of our social behavior is based on what we see portrayed in media.

Human beings use their sixth sense every second of the day. We even use it in our sleep. Without my sixth sense, I would not be able to function in my daily life. Almost a decade of listening to how intangible energy feels, I have refined my extra sensory, sentient ability, which we all share. I am not psychic. I just listen better. Anyone can, if they care enough to pay attention. I do not watch television, and I am not a movie goer. The only memories I had of what Robin Williams looked like were from the 1970's. Robin's physical appearance before he passed away was a lot different than how he looked when he was in his thirty's. When I came across the alias "R. William Rheineschild" on the property records of one of Cindy McCain's buildings, It felt the same as Michael Sherman. Except the feeling was not the same as the Michael Sherman, I met through Cecy Groom in Beverly Hills. Around February 2014, I discovered evidence suggesting Michael Sherman was an impersonator known for his signature role as "Ed Sullivan." I now know that was a distraction.

By removing myself and taking a step back, the perspective is slightly insulting. Every aspect of society has hierarchy. Regardless of the angle, I will always be "Alejandro" which by default places me at the top of that hierarchy. At the bottom are the impersonators, next to the catfish and politicians. There will always be one original and many copies. The fact that in this case, the copies overstepped their social position and believed they would have the advantage based on the fact they outnumber the originals was, without better words, optimistically delusional.

When one establishes himself as being an Original, the reason is beyond the superficial. I was responsible for allowing them to exploit me. The reason, and I will be honest, was because I wanted to be able to fuck them using their own fists. They made an effort to harm me. Whether they acted in malice is beside the point. It is the principle that matters to me. At the end of the day, the number of carbon copies flooding the media is irrelevant because when people meet me, there is no mistake that I am the original. To prove it, I have kept records every time I come across one of my doubles. I have saved each misappropriation. The following images, combined with all the other images in this book, are not even a drop in the bucket. I am so confident that I have mixed my real images among the look-a-likes. A hundred years from now, when we are all dead and gone, the world will know I was "Alejandro."

That is what they gave me, and it is priceless. But, before I continue, I have to specify that I am not "Mexican." My mother is Sefardic Jew, French and Spanish and my father is Saudi, Italian and Spanish. The only connection between my family's lineage to Mexico, is through our ancestor

Don Alfonso de Estrada, Duque of Aragon and son of King Ferdinand ll of Aragon who was appointed as the Royal Proxie over New Spain. Our family was forced to abandon our titles during the Mexican revolution. That is how my family ended up in California. There might be many lines of Estrada, however, our line carries the "Holy Grail" O Rh negative blood type. The "Blood of Jesus" and it can be traced back to the Merovigian Dynasty. Coincidentally, my maternal grandfather was also O RH negative. Anyone may disbelieve me, however, no one can argue with the science.

| Search | | search | games | help | invite | music | ▶ | log out |

Alex Estrada

Alex Estrada

Birthday:	October 2, 1994
Hometown:	Queens, New York
Relationship status:	Single
Studied at:	Georgian Court University '16
Languages:	English, Español

Hide full information

Contact information

Current city:	Lakewood
Mobile:	732-773-4666
Skype:	PAPI10292

Education

College or university:	Georgian Court University '16
Department:	School of Sciences and Mathematics
Major:	Sociology, Anthropology and Criminal Justice
School:	Lakewood High School '12 Lakewood

Send a message

Add to friends

Send a gift

Block Alex
Report profile

Personal information

No information.

4 photos see all

2 posts

Alex Estrada

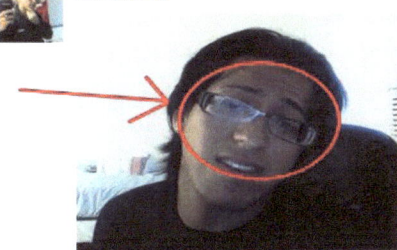

12 Jun 2012 | Comment   Like

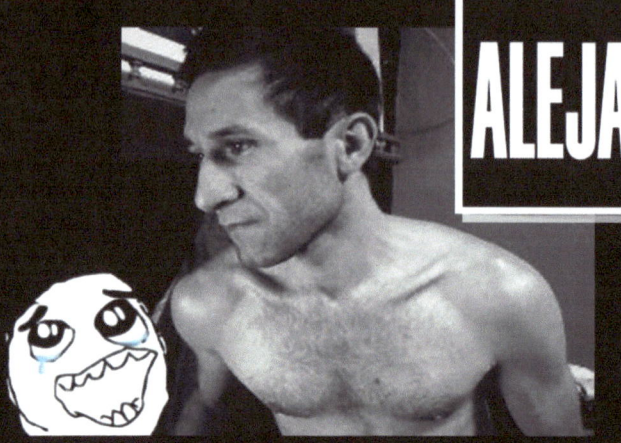

ALEJANDRO

I know that we are young and I know that you may love me

But I just can't be with you like this anymore

Michael R. Goss
April 18, 1953 - February 14, 2009

Don't call my name
Don't call my name
ALEJANDRO

Don't wanna kiss
Don't wanna touch
just smoke my cigarette and hush

ALEJANDRO
Stop
Please
Just let me go
Alejandro
Just let me go

efforts of 77 Los Angeles Firefighters,

Fire loss is estimated at $380,000

Now he's gonna find a fight gonna fool the bad

nothing to lose

will sign a letter to never talk or bring up any of

90: He's not that involved,

New York a 3:28 PM , but you risk 95%

Dubai and Washington DC

Mossad

Jew!

Lady Gaga Cancels Tour for Hip Surgery

CELEBRITY NEWS FEBR FEBRUARY 14, 2013

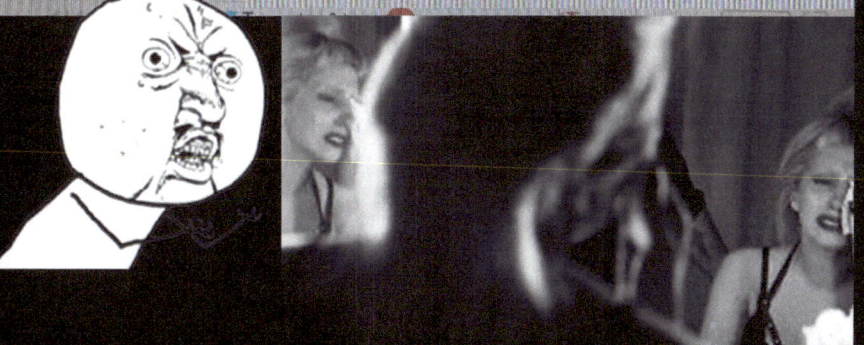

WANTED
BY THE FBI

Failure to Appear

XUYEN THI-KIM NGUYEN

Aliases:
Thi Kim Nguyen, Kim Nguyen, Xuyen Nguyen

DESCRIPTION

Date(s) of Birth Used:	February 16, 1942	**Hair:**	Black
Place of Birth:	Vietnam	**Eyes:**	Brown
Height:	5'0"	**Sex:**	Female
Weight:	135 pounds	**Race:**	Asian
NCIC:	W175683980	**Nationality:**	Vietnamese
Occupation:	Unknown		

Scars and Marks: None known
Remarks: Nguyen became a naturalized citizen in 1999. She has lived in the Seattle, Washington, and Dallas, Texas, areas.

CAUTION

In May 2005, seven individuals, including Xuyen Thi-Kim Nguyen, were indicted in Dallas, Texas, for their involvement in a scheme to defraud a mortgage company of over $5 million. After four of the seven individuals pled guilty, Nguyen was convicted of one count of conspiracy, two counts of mail fraud, and seven counts of fraud by wire. Nguyen was placed on home monitoring until her sentencing. However, some time between November 8, 2005, and November 11, 2005, Nguyen fled from her home in Plano, Texas. Subsequently, a complaint was filed in the Northern District of Texas for failure to appear, and an arrest warrant was issued by the United States District Court on February 3, 2006.

If you have any information concerning this person, please contact your local FBI office or the nearest American Embassy or Consulate.

PORN GODS

WHORE HAUS INVADES HOCROD

HALLOWEEN PARTY

WEDNESDAY OCTOBER 29

HOSTED BY
SAINT PETER D'VII
NOTORIOUS ALI DOOM

NO COVER

GUEST HOSTS:
JUDAS JOE MANSON AND DAKOTA D'VII
DJ JOHNNY JEWEL

DRAG PERFORMANCES THROUGHOUT THE NIGHT

MICKY'S — 8857 SANTA MONICA BLVD

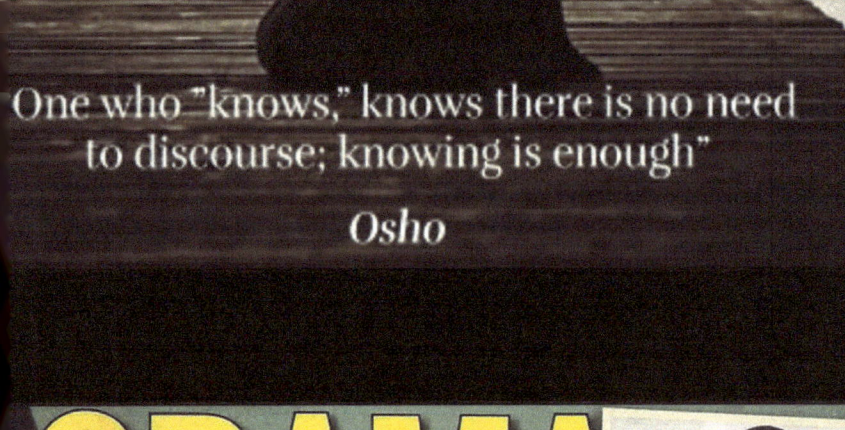

One who "knows," knows there is no need to discourse; knowing is enough"

Osho

OBAMA GAY SCANDAL!

NEW details in blockbuster book

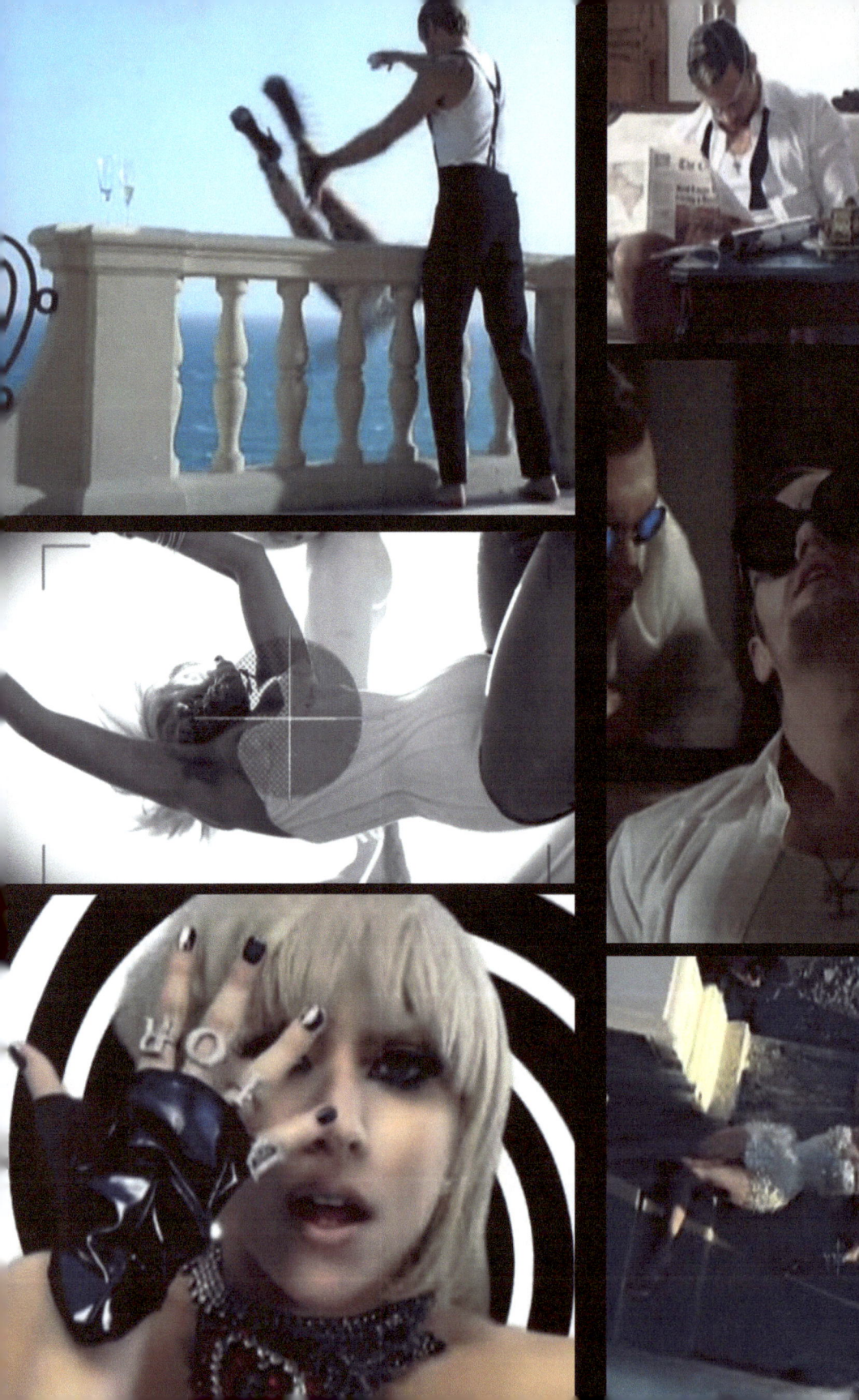

Mark Combs

My Achilles Heel

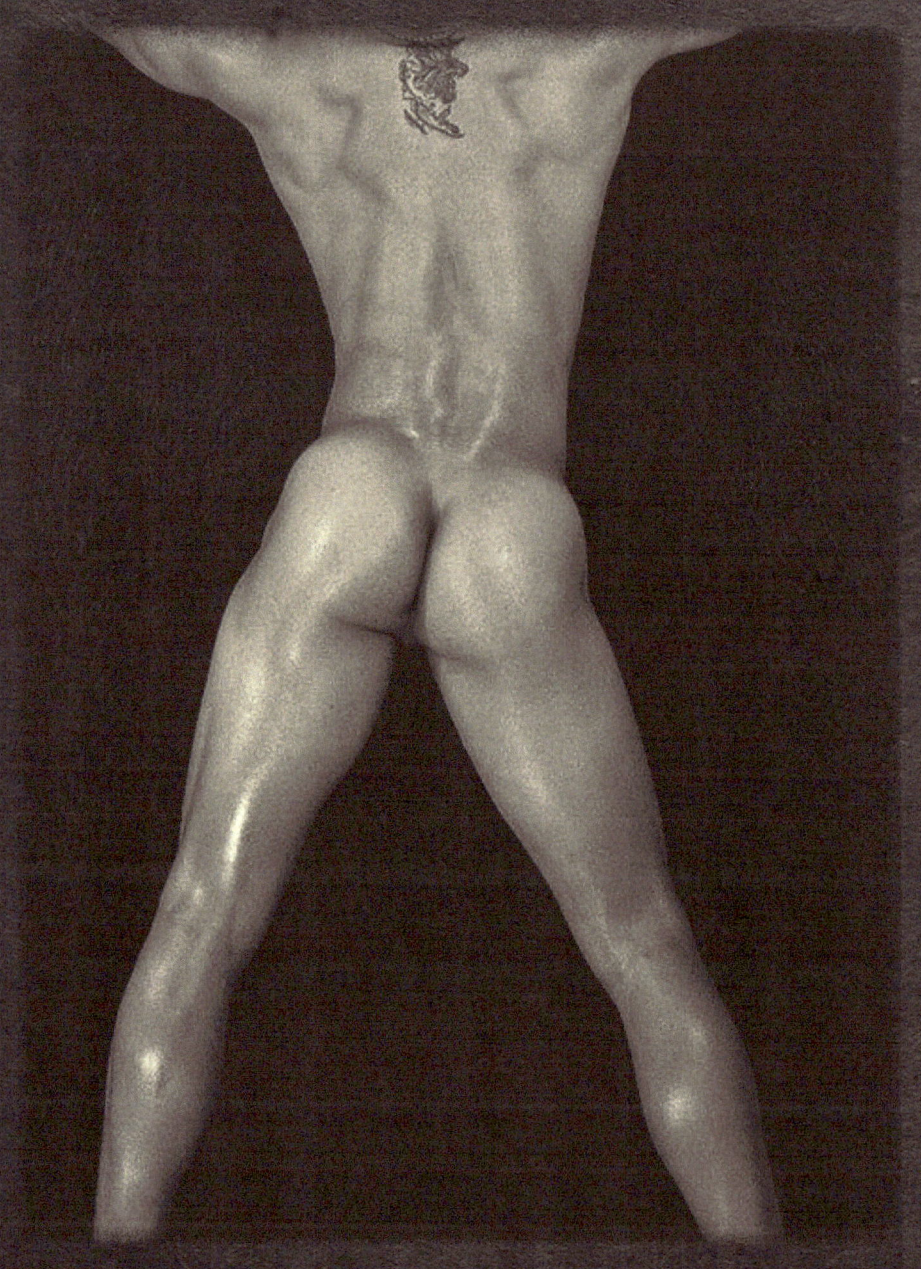

In this existence, nothing is more captivating than the physical beauty found only in the male of our species. In my opinion, the beauty of the male gender is divine, and this divinity is like a rose reaching up towards a state of perfection that once achieved, withers rapidly and then is lost forever. Mark Combs was the most beautiful boy I ever dreamed of; if I could have stopped time just to lose myself in each second of him, it would not have been long enough. When we made love, I could feel his heart pounding throughout my entire body. As he inhaled, I would exhale and for that moment we were one; as if suspended together in heaven. We spent days driving through California, completely lost not knowing where we were. Stupid in love. Exploring the California deserts along unpaved roads; making love on top of the car with only the moon and stars to blanket us, everything was perfect in my life as long as Mark was next to me.

At the time, my work was seasonal, and my schedule kept me on the road for the duration of the season. I had no choice but to return him to his family. According to his story, Mark was a foster child whose father murdered his mother. Cindy McCain was supposed to be his foster guardian, whom he referred to as "Kathy." In chapter seven of my first book I referenced her by the name "Cathy Kutzner." I have verified the identities of the people Mark Combs called his "grandparents" as Cindy McCain's parents.

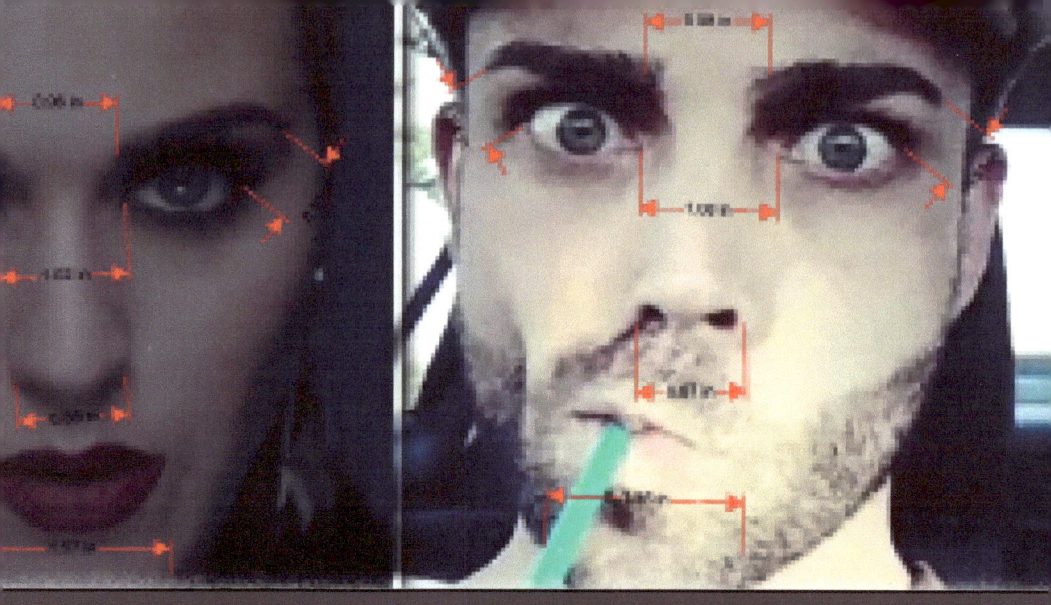

They owned a home in Fullerton, California that sat on an acre lot complete with an orchard grove. Mark had a minor car accident and the car stayed parked at my place until it could be towed to Fullerton. Eventually, the car was towed. Mark's foster guardian's husband was John, and he called numerous times regarding the car keys. Mark gave me a silver rabbit ring that he said belonged to his mother, for safe keeping. The rabbit symbol held sentimental value. On his arm, he even had tattoo of a rabbit in remembrance of his mother. I still have that ring, and I found it odd that he never asked for it back. The last time we spoke was in San Diego the following year. We arranged to meet, but he never showed up. I do not know what became of Mark; he seemed to have dropped off the face of the earth. Most people would know Mark by the name Katy Perry. There is a chance he is no longer alive because at the present, the person claiming to be Katy Perry, is not the same person that made the name Katy Perry famous.

A L E J A N D R O

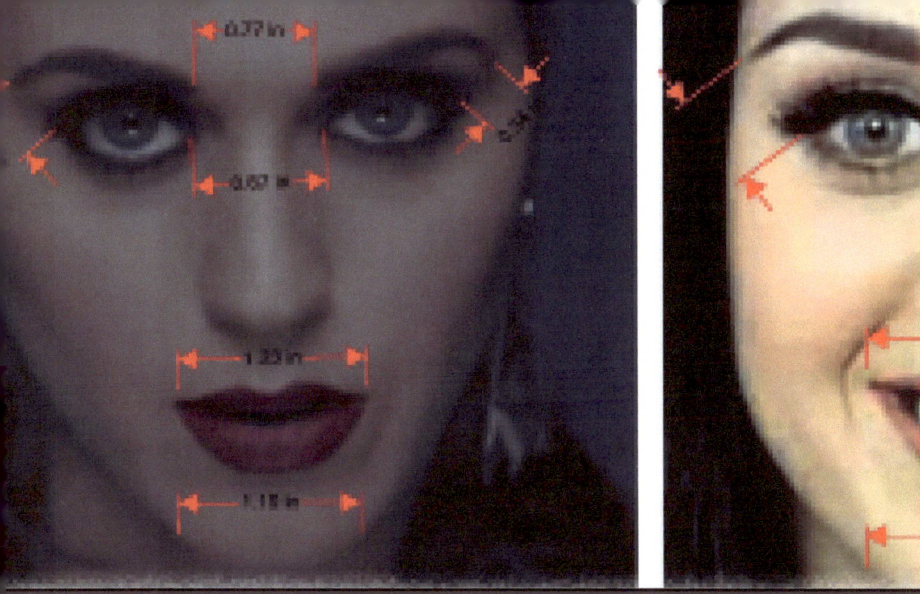

The most blatant reference to my relationship with Mark is in the music video for "Hot and Cold." My character's name is "Alexander" and I have reason to believe two other music videos make subtle references to me. For instance, the video for "Thinking of You" depicts my character as a World War II soldier who gets shot and killed during battle. Then, in the music video for "The one that got Away" my character dies in a car accident. Mark and I met the summer after he graduated high school, so the lyrics "The summer after high school when we first met" is difficult. One of the characters in the music video for the song "Happy Birthday" is an animal trainer named "ACE." My initials are ACE. ACE is also my pseudonym and the acronym for Anti-Christ Endowments. The music video for "Dark Horse" is about Cindy McCain's sacrificial appetite and control of the music industry. She uses fear to control her music artists.

A L E J A N D R O

Most people are not aware that rap artist Snoop Dogg is one of her business partners. He has an office in Newport Beach California, which is referred to as "The Golden Coast." "The Golden Coast" is also a reference to the location of his New Jersey office. Many consumers have no idea how the music industry operates. Contracts between artist and label enslave or indenture the music artist. Non-disclosure clauses limit the artist's freedom of speech. These contracts specify what they can and cannot discuss, and what they are allowed to say during interviews with the media.

Overstepping the limits of the contract make them liable for breach of contract. Except, lawsuits fall under arbitration to ensure the privacy of the contract details. The artist runs the risk of losing the money they made while working under the contract if the record label files a lawsuit for breaching the contract. The other purpose of arbitration is to give the Studio the legal advantage.

The fame and media coverage the artists receive becomes a debt they owe to their record label, and they work off that debt by making music and performing. Everything the artist creates becomes the property of the music label. From my understanding, Sony Music Publishing currently controls the music industry. In most cases, the music artists never pays off that debt and even after the death of a music artist; a record label continues making money off them. The public is not meant to see the ugly truth once the camera lights go dark. These contracts are private. It is not uncommon for contracts to include unwritten clauses regarding the artist's sexual conduct. Whether they are expected to give favorable treatment and if so, to whom they are expected not to say "no" to. Many of these artists are under the age of legal consent. The lucky ones have parents that protect them. Unfortunately, the majority do not.

It is a typical scenario, where one parent coaches the artist to extend sexual favors, for example, to a manager or agent. The objective is to acquire the leverage to use as blackmail. Most of these parents do not have the advanced legal degrees required to go head to head with the power attorneys at the record label or studio. Blackmail, is often the only option they have to maintain some advantage. Even then, the artist still ends up a victim. Then there are some situations, when the consequence is death. In the music industry, hookers end up dead, and they disappear.

That sends a very clear message.

When I introduced Mark Combs to Michael Sherman (Robin Williams), Robin took an immediate interest in him. Everyone did. Mark was a singer studying music at Cal State Northridge. Some of my fondest memories of Mark are singing parts with him. Although, my experience with other singers had not been as positive. Immediately after being accepted as a Young American, the director Milton Brown, invited me to record. Milton took me under his wing as a protégé. Our first rehearsal someone in the tenor section was off. I kind of panicked. It had to be me, right? Well, it was not me. Milton put us all on the spot by making each one of us take turns singing our part accapella. There were maybe five of us that day. I was second to go. The song was "Swing on a Star" and by the time I got to the second bar, the entire room was fixed on me. As I continued, the resentment increased. By the time I finished, the hatred was burning my skin. That was when it began. It almost became violent. Half way through the recording I had to stop, and I never looked back.

That particular recording was reserved only for the members with the most seniority. My peers had already bonded as cast members and they singled me out. I had been around long enough to know that was not a situation I wanted to deal with, and it was so traumatic for me, I decided not to sing in public ever again. Except singing is part of who I am. I needed to sing, like a canary sings to feel the air rushing over his wings, from inside a cage. Chapman University has an excellent music department, and I resumed my Opera training with Robin Buck. Chapman University offered me a music scholarship, but my curriculum could not accommodate the added class requirements. Besides, I never wanted a career as a singer because for me; singing is more private than my nudity. It is a gift I share intimately with the people closest to me.

I met with Robin Buck at the same time Professor Hall, the Chair of the Music Department, was conducting a workshop. During one of our sessions, I was singing "Why God" from the musical Miss Saigon. When I hit the "A" note at the end of the piece, the windows started humming, and Professor Hall walked out of his lecture. He just stood there in the corridor. When I finished, he walked in and asked Robin Buck who "his student" was. It was humiliating. Once a year the Opera Department produced a medley, except I was never invited to participate. There was no mistake I had the ability to sing Opera, but having the ability is one thing. Whether or not it is pleasant to listen to, is another thing. I felt that if I had been good enough, the department would have given me the opportunity to participate.

I am my worst critic, and as critics go, I'm unforgiving.

The last time I sang was in Palm Springs. Michael Goss used the house as a filming studio, so the acoustics were superb. A month before leaving on hiatus, I was subjected to a whole new level of mistreatment. It has not stopped. I became a whipping boy. I was not allowed to participate in any of the social gatherings, and while everyone was partying together at another house, I sang " Close Every Door" from the musical Joseph. After my shower, I noticed one of the cameras had been left on.

Michael Goss was also a Young American, and like the rest of them, he hated me for my voice. The man was unable to handle himself appropriately whenever I sang, and every morning I do my Opera warm-up in the shower. I felt like he was punishing me each time I opened my mouth. I did not need that extra stress. Especially considering the people surrounding him were not our " friends." That was causing me to suffer panic attacks from the anxiety the intentions of that cabal, were causing me. Michael Goss kept telling me I was just paranoid. Meanwhile, he kept putting me through it. Consequently, now I know why caged birds sing, except I am too fucked up with PTSD to even hum. I decided to leave on hiatus, because the situation digressed to such a level of insanity that one night I walked to the Palm Springs Airport and booked a seat on the next flight to Los Angeles. That weekend we drove his car. He had no idea I left. The next flight out was the following morning. By that time, it was 9pm, and I had no cash on me. I had to walk my ass back, in the dark because I was too proud to have him pay for my cab. When I left, he had three house guests, by the time I got back they had grown to 10 house guests; doing what gay men do best. I will never forget what Michael told me that night. He said

> "*I NEED YOU IN MY LIFE, AS PART OF MY LIFE. MY HOME IS YOUR HOME, EVERY LAST ONE OF MY HOMES BELONG TO YOU. THEY ARE OUR HOMES. DO NOT EVER FEEL UNWELCOME, IN OUR HOME.*"

And I knew I fucked up because every vulture, circling overhead, heard him say it. The following week someone broke into the house in Palm Springs. I wanted to hire an armed private guard but because that was "paranoid" I settled for having the Alarm system reactivated. He promised me he would get that done. Except when I needed it, the service was not available. It might sound like paranoia when I claim someone has been hunting me since 2008. But, no psychiatrist can diagnose me as suffering from paranoia because if it were a delusion, no one would be dead. Michael Goss would still be alive. Lina Morgana would still be alive, and this book would not exist.

censoring the details surrounding her murder. All the while, Lady Gaga's creative team, producers, and record label have been exploiting those details. The events surrounding Ms. Morgana's tragic murder ended up being reenacted in the music video for the song "Paparazzi." Lina Morgana's case was brought to my attention in August of 2014. I made an effort to reach out to Ms. Morgana's surviving relatives. I wanted to obtain their permission for including her in this book. Unfortunately, those requests have gone unanswered. My knowledge of Lina Morgana's life and death is limited to information found in the public domain. I have not had the time to verify the information with the State Assessor's office. With that said, I do believe someone murdered Ms. Morgana. I know from my life experience how the two favorite ways to cover-up homicide is by using "suicide" or "Cancer" as the cause of death. Keep in mind, in real life, the only people with the credentials to challenge a medical diagnosis are medical doctors. Medicine is a profession where medical doctors take an oath to protect the interests of their fellow peers. Therefore, doctors will never testify against another physician, nor will any doctor turn in another doctor for murder. When a doctor commits murder, the reason is limited to the cause of death or malpractice. In malpractice cases, insurance agents determine fault based on established medical protocols. Based on privileged information, I know that someone still wants to use me as a sacrificial offering.

It is an odd coincidence that Stephani Germanotta and I were both born at the same time and we share the same celebrity because I believe, I was the only sacrifice they could not complete.

Mystic energy is always two sided, like a ying and a yang. If fame were acquired through mystic channels then it would explain how my celebrity is the mirror opposite from Lady Gaga's celebrity. Although, without me, Lady Gaga would not be famous; and without Lady Gaga, I would not be a void of fame. Life may not be fair, but the universe is. To even out the balance of power, I am allowed to write this book and expose these crimes so that one day, when my opposition is no longer alive to roadblock me, the world might finally know the truth. Then, once the illusion has faded and the deception disappears, balance can be returned to normal.

The most valuable thing anyone could have given me was Inclusion except now, inclusion has become meaningless because essentially, no one chooses anything uncommon, unless they too are such.

Inclusion, was never meant for me and a thousand lives from this one, I will still yearn for it because now that I have voiced it, I will never be able to trust it. Therefore, I am grateful that the people targeting me are wealthy enough to afford my retribution. Although, that will never happen because justice in "America" does not exist.

Letters and Memos

The following dialog is from a conversation I had with Judas Joe Manson, whose real name is Gabriel Cordero

ACE	I hope you would agree and if you want to know the truth, I can give it to you
	What's up
ACE	Do you know who owns 847 Hammond Street?
	Umm no ?
ACE	his name was Michael Goss he was murdered
	Ok? What are you talking about ? How does this tie with me?
ACE	Because according to your bank statement, you're living at 847 Hammond Street unless of course someone is trying to set you up
	What are you talking about what bank statement? The picture you sent me isn't even my name
ACE	"Judas Joe Manson" is Joseph Manson. it's the same name
	Not really lol thank you though and why would you have my bank state? If it was mine.

ACE: OK well here's a heads up .... using an alias is ok [as a stage name] however using an alias [as your identity] for legal reasons, (such as opening a ban account) is considered fraud ... I found your [bank] statement on the dining room table at 847 Hammond Street... I'm "Alejandro", that's my house and I have legal access to that property... I also have the legal right to report any trespassing, but I do not have the energy to deal with all that drama

What's an alias? So because "MANSON" is apart of the name your thinking I'm trespassing or under an alias?

ACE: Because the property is involved in a homicide investigation anyone found on the property other than the property owner would be considered an accomplice to murder and co conspirator

We'll honey boo I'm way to busy to try & kill someone .. Thank you though

ACE: I never said you killed anyone

& about the pictures you tagged me too .. Is that like just a collage you decided to do or?...

ACE: Its being published in my new book so you might want to let your attorney know

Like the Gaga images, my images & all the others? May I know why your using my images?

ACE: Because you are living in my house. It seems fair

A L E J A N D R O

> Your house? What are you talking about?

ACE: 847 Hammond Street

> Ok Alex I don't live at that address .. I don't even speak to you what makes you think you can try & even accuse me of living somewhere & use my images because you think I do?

ACE: OK so then who is Joe Manson? Is that Stefano Russo?

> Ok .. Your talking nonsense .. When you learn what a nick name "stage name" is You'll answer your own question .. Till then don't use my images for any of your projects last thing we need is a tiff .. I don't know you & you don't know me "AT ALL"

ACE: You're the only Joe Manson I have been able to find ..... unless Stefano Russo is playing games which is what it feels like but whatever the case is, I'm sure it'll all get sorted out somehow

> Your not making SENSE dude

ACE: Joesph Manson. in a court of law, that is the same name as Joe Manson and the fact that I am "Alejandro" it makes [the situation] look really fucked up [A Lady Gaga impersonator living in the house of the person who Lady Gaga named the song "Alejandro" after)

> Your talking about Stefano & about me living in your house?! Who in the fuck are you?

A L E J A N D R O

ACE	So one of you will have to sue me ... when the book is released I'll send you copy. BTW I would love for someone to explain the connection between Russo, Cecy Groom and Zelda Williams
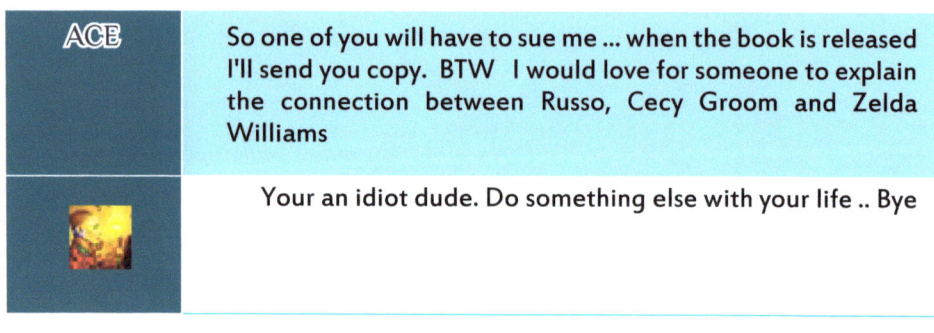	Your an idiot dude. Do something else with your life .. Bye

Memo to LASD

TO:	LASD, WEST HOLLYWOOD STATION DETECTIVE UNIT TEL: 310-855-8850 ext 560 FAX: 310-659-4589
	KATHERINE GORRIS, PRIVACY MANAGER CEDARS-SINAI TEL: 323-866-7877
FROM:	ALEJANDRO ESTRADA, SURVIVING RELATIVE OF ALLEGED HOMICIDE VICTIM MICHAEL R. GOSS OF 847 HAMMOND STREET IN WEST HOLLYWOOD
SUBJECT	INQUIRY INTO THE DEATH OF MICHAEL RITO GOSS [VICTIM] AND REQUEST FOR INVESTIGATION
DATE	October 31, 2014
CC	FEDERAL BUREAU OF INVESTIGATION, DALLAS LOCAL OFFICE [see attached]

A request for a regulatory review and official assessment of the Death Certificate belonging to Michael Rito Goss of 847 Hammond Street in the city of West Hollywood, signed by Cedars Sinai physician Ian Robert Goodman, M.D. [Board License #A81768]. Dr. Goodman failed to follow medical and CDC protocol for reporting cause of death. According to Dr. Goodman, Mr. Goss's immediate cause of death was "metastatic renal cell carcinoma" however according to independent physician consultations Dr. Goodman inaccurately recorded his diagnosis and may have committed a crime by doing so. There is also a discrepancy of at least 12 hours from the last time Mr. Goss was seen alive, which was on February 13, 2009, and his time of death at exactly 12:00 PM on February 14, 2009. Not only did Mr. Goss NOT have cancer, the alleged cremation was not desired by Mr. Goss which is a violation of both Federal and California State laws. ***Pursuant to California State Code 102220: The State Registrar shall carefully examine the certificates received from the local registrars of births, deaths, and fetal deaths, and if they are incomplete or unsatisfactory shall require any further information that may be necessary to make the record complete and satisfactory. (b) Notwithstanding Section 126 of the Penal Code, the crime of Perjury specified in paragraph (4) of subdivision (b) of Section 102230, paragraph (6) of subdivision (c) of Section 102230, and subdivision (b) of Section 102231, shall be punishable as a misdemeanor

Therefore, in pursuant to California Penal Code Sections 182, 182.5, 186.22, 132-34 as well as Civil Procedure Section 377.60-377.62 subsection 4.1.1 a homicide investigation is warranted, lawful and required by state law.

- The Real Estate Fraud being committed against Mr. Goss's estate is estimated to exceed the monetary value of $1 Million and both the Riverside and Los Angeles county District Attorney offices have been notified.
- The events surrounding Mr. Goss's mysterious death suggest Mr. Goss and his partner, Mr. Estrada, were targeted by a conspiracy to commit murder which based on forensic evidence in Mr. Estrada's possession, is believed to have been conspired by

CECY GROOM	FLORA NAVARRO	CARMELITA LAMPINO
12157 ST TROPEZ DRIVE	11033 E. ROSECRANS	17702 CALIENTE PL
CERRITOS, CA 90703	AVE, STE.D	CERRITOS, CA 90703
	NORWALK, CA 90650	

Be advised, the real property located at 847 Hammond Street is unlawfully occupied by trespassers who Mr. Estrada has never met. These trespassers have not been given authorization by Mr. Estrada or the late Mr. Goss and they are occupying this residence by force. California Penal Code Section 602 defines this as aggravated criminal trespassing and should be filed as a felony. Numerous requests have been made to enforce this law which the LASD continues to ignore and\or censor. In addition to aggravated trespassing, these individuals have destroyed three large trees growing on the property which violates Penal Code Section 602. Moreover they have done so without obtaining permission or filing the appropriate permits to do so and they have acted in malice because Mr. Goss was closely attached to these trees.

At this time, Mr. Estrada is also requesting proof of transfer of Mr. Goss's body from Cedar Sinai to the crematory facility listed on the death certificate and proof of payment of that transfer. Kindly be aware Probate for Mr. Goss's Estate has not been discharged because the Successor Trustee DOES NOT exist and probate was filed numerous times which further

A L E J A N D R O

implicates these suspects for having committed perjury and fraud against the State of California. [LASC BP-115442 and LASC BP-119874] Forensic analysis and examination is currently being performed, however, the State of California has more than enough evidence to file criminal charges and open a homicide investigation.

The Michael R. Goss Living Trust, dated Februar 2009

By: Thomas J. Proechel, Trustee

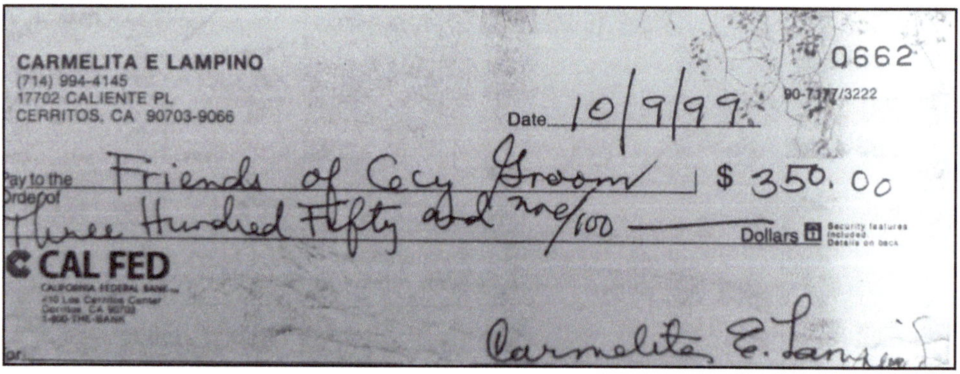

CARMELITA E LAMPINO
(714) 994-4145
17702 CALIENTE PL
CERRITOS, CA 90703-9066

0662
90-7377/3222

Date 10/9/99

Pay to the Order of Friends of Cocy Groom $ 350.00

Three Hundred Fifty and no/100 ———— Dollars

CAL FED
CALIFORNIA FEDERAL BANK

Carmelita E. Lampino

We also declare that at the time of our attestation of this Will, Michael R. Goss w
our best knowledge and belief, of sound mind and memory, eighteen years of age o
and under no duress, menace, fraud, misrepresentation, constraint or undue influenc

Executed on February 13, 2009 in the County of Los Angeles, California.

_____
Jan Morrison, Witness
2800 Neilson Way, Suite 709
Santa Monica, CA 90405

_____
Nicole Gallardo, Witness
2800 Neilson Way, Suite 4
Santa Monica, CA 90405

FLORA S. MOTUS
TRUSTEE FOR THE MOTUS FAMILY LIVING
TRUST DTD NOVEMBER 26 - 1991
11125 HIBBING ST.
CERRITOS, CA 90703

90-8186/1211
673861043

184

Date 10-10-99

Pay to the Order of: Friends of Ceci Groom $ 50.XX/100

Fifty dollars & XX/100   Dollars

WORLD SAVINGS®
BANK, FSB
11400 East South Street
Cerritos, California 90703

Memo _____   Flora S. Motus

A L E J A N D R O

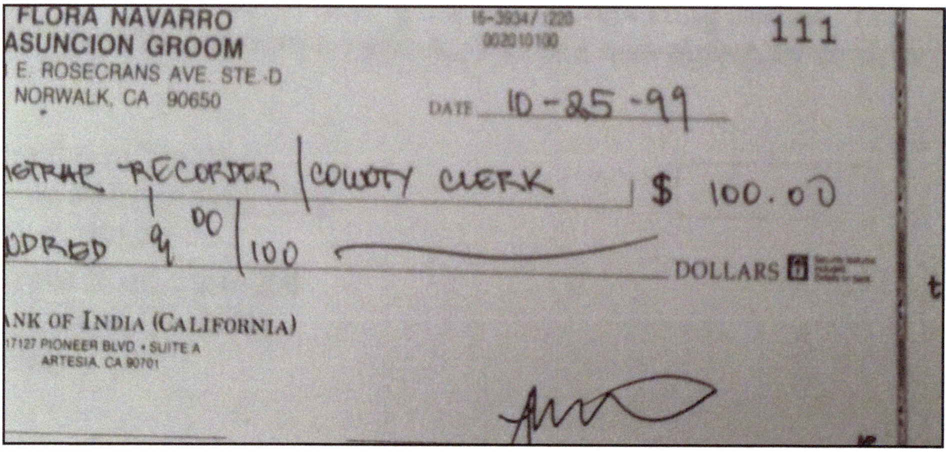

142

FLORA NAVARRO	16-3634/1220	111
ASUNCION GROOM	002010100	
E. ROSECRANS AVE. STE-D		
NORWALK, CA 90650	DATE 10-25-99	

ISTRAR RECORDER / COUNTY CLERK $ 100.00

...DRED 9 00/100 _____ DOLLARS

...NK OF INDIA (CALIFORNIA)
17127 PIONEER BLVD. • SUITE A
ARTESIA, CA 90701

Michael R. Goss, Assignor

ALEJANDRO

_____
Michael R. Goss

_____
ael R. Goss, Grantor and Trustee

American Express Bank, FSB
P.O. Box 30384
Salt Lake City, UT 84130-0384

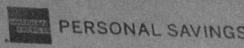 PERSONAL SAVINGS

JOSEPH S MANSON
847 HAMMOND ST
WEST HOLLYWOOD, CA 90069

For questions please call: 1-800-437-3600

PAYER'S name, address, and telephone number AMERICAN EXPRESS BANK, FSB P.O. BOX 30384 SALT LAKE CITY, UT 84130-0384	Payer's RTN (optional)	OMB No. 1545-0112
	1 Interest income	**2013** Form **1099-INT**	Interest Income
	2 Early withdrawal penalty		
PAYER'S federal identification number	RECIPIENT'S identification number	3 Interest on U.S. Savings Bonds and Treas. obligations	Copy B For Recipient This is important tax information and is being furnished to the Internal Revenue Service. If you are required to file a return, a negligence penalty or other sanction may be imposed on you if this income is taxable and the IRS determines that it has not been reported.
RECIPIENT'S name, and address JOSEPH S MANSON 847 HAMMOND ST WEST HOLLYWOOD, CA 90069	4 Federal income tax withheld	5 Investment expenses	
	6 Foreign tax paid	7 Foreign country or U.S. possession	
	8 Tax-exempt interest	9 Specified private activity bond interest	
Account number (see instructions) See Details Below	10 Tax-exempt bond CUSIP no.	11 State	12 State identification no.	13 State tax withheld

Form 1099-INT (keep for your records) Department of the Treasury - Internal Revenue Service

See Details

ACCOUNT NUMBER	INTEREST INCOME	EARLY WITHDRAWAL PENALTY	FEDERAL INCOME TAX WITHHELD

Memo to Riverside County DA

5/3/2013
FROM: Alejandro Estrada
TO: LARRY W. WARD - COUNTY OF RIVERSIDE ASSESSOR
RIVERSIDE COUNTY DISTRICT ATTORNEY - REAL ESTATE FRAUD
Assessor
P.O. Box 12004
Riverside, CA 92502-2204 Tel. (951) 955-6200

Riverside County District Attorney - Real Estate Fraud Unit

I am contacting your office to report real estate fraud in connection to a possible homicide, which is regarding Los Angeles County Superior Court Probate case file BP 115442, The Michael R. Goss Living Trust. Please be advised, I have filed multiple criminal complaints against Mr. Thomas Proechel, the Successor Trustee for the estate belonging to Michael R. Goss. Michael Goss's death was made to appear as if he died from cancer. Not only did Michael Goss not have cancer, but according to Cedars Sinai Medical Center's Legal Affairs department, Michael Goss was not one of their patients. I know this, because I met with a representative at Cedars Sinai after Mr. Proechel filed a second fraudulent probate case. Los Angeles County Superior Court case file BP 119874 was filed exparte wherein Mr. Proechel claimed to be acting on behalf of Cedars Sinai as a creditor on the basis of collecting Michael Goss' Medi-Cal benefits in order to pay a past due hospital bill. Mr. Proechel's misconduct has been unbelievable and this are just an example of the discrepancies which contribute to my suspicion.

Mr. Proechel's most recent criminal transaction involves the property at 2557 S. Broadmoor Drive in Palm Springs, which was held in trust by the Michael R. Goss Living Trust and is currently in probate. 2557 South Broadmoor Drive, in Palm Springs [Parcel ID # 681222018] was listed for $389,000.00 [MLS# 12632767] by a Mr. Mark Dubas [DRE #: 01908786] with Coldwell Banker. Please note Mr. Dubas and Mr. Proechel's contact information below.

Mark E. Dubas	Thomas Proechel	Jan Morrison
1611 Electric Ave, Venice, CA, 90291 Office Phone: (424) 280-7400 Cell Phone: (310) 922-2009 Fax: (424) 280-7404 Email: Mark.Dubas@coldwellbanker.com	2800 Neilson Way Apartment 709 Santa Monica, CA 90405 *Mr. Proechel relocated to this address after the Court informed him, he was violating Probate code by living at 847 Hammond Street. He moved in to my home after he locked me out.	Attorney at Law 2800 Neilson Way Apartment 709 Santa Monica, 90405 *Jan Morrison is the Attorney for the estate.

On March 5, 2013, the aforesaid property sold for $380,000.00, however, Mr. Proechel transferred ownership of the property from the Michael R. Goss Trust, into his own name. Mr. Dubas' ethics are disconcerting and his action of listing a property in probate, and the effort of making that transaction seem legitimate, could implicate him for being an accomplice to Mr. Proechel; especially considering that it seems as if no monetary transaction took place.

There is something horribly wrong with this case and I have conducted my own investigation because Los Angeles County District Attorney's office has been covering up these illegalities. Therefore, do not expect the Los Angeles District Attorney to cooperate because according to Mr. Cooley, the $10 million plus value of the Michael Goss' estate, does not meet the $300,000.00 prerequisite for the DA to open an investigation.

A L E J A N D R O

Memo to Marin County

Memorandum

After careful examination, Mr. Alejandro Estrada believes he knew Mr. Robin Williams by the name "Michael Sherman" and is bringing the following information to the attention of the Marin County Sheriffs in response to the investigation into the death of actor Robin Williams.

On May 21, 2014 Mr. Estrada confronted Mr. Williams regarding his alias with the following message:

> "Do you realize that I would have to have been mentally impaired or clinically insane to believe any of you would help me? Because this goes so far past gullible it becomes malicious. I don't care about the deception because my sixth sense knows better, but what I find disappointing is how all the people in my life believe I'm a retarded eunuch who doesn't know the difference between a glory hole and a urinal..... "

Mr. Williams responded via email with the message "Correct" dated June 12, 2014.

Then, on June 16, 2014, Mr. Estrada sent an email to Mr. Michael Aquino, MD that read

> "I THINK YOUR SON'S LAW FIRM IN VIENNA SHOULD DRAFT UP A CONTRACT BECAUSE RREEF GLOBAL INC. HAS A CORPORATE HEADQUARTERS IN AUSTRIA WHICH QUALIFIES FOR JURISDICTION RIGHTS. THE FIRM IN MANHATTAN IS CONNECTING TOO MANY DOTS AND THEY'RE PRESSURING ME TO GIVE MY CONSENT FOR USING MY EVIDENCE IN PROCEEDINGS TO IMPEACH OBAMA. APPARENTLY THERE WERE SOME MURDERS IN CHICAGO THAT ARE LINKED TO HIM. I FEEL THEY [CINDY MCCAIN ET AL] ARE TRYING TO DIMINISH MY CLAIM BUT IF THAT'S THE ONLY OPTION I HAVE THEN I WILL HAVE NO CHOICE IN THE MATTER REALLY. I WOULD RATHER SETTLE OUT OF COURT FOR [REDACTED] BESIDES I DON'T BELIEVE THE AMERICAN SOCIETY WILL BE ABLE TO HANDLE THIS MUCH REALITY AND WHO KNOWS WHAT WOULD HAPPEN IF IT HIT THE PRESS. RIGHT NOW THE FIRM HAS THEIR HANDS TIED BECAUSE I TOOK THE PRECAUTION TO INCLUDE A JOURNALIST FOR TRANSPARENCY. HOWEVER, I WOULD RATHER BE COMPENSATED [FOR THE PAIN AND SUFFERING] AND MOVE ON WITH MY BROKEN LIFE."

Neither Mr. Williams or Mr. Aquino responded, nor was any attempt made by Mr. Estrada to contact them. In light of Mr. Williams's recent death, Mr. Estrada is submitting forensic evidence that could prove Mr. Williams and Mr. Aquino were both playing the role of was "Mr. Sherman" in order to sabotage the homicide investigation into the death of Mr. Estrada's partner, Michael Rito Goss.

Mr. Estrada identifies the man on the right as Mr. Sherman and the young woman on the left as someone he met by the name "Tara." The same young woman is seen in this photograph As Ms. Michelle Groom while standing next to former Congressional Candidate Mrs. Cecy Groom of Groom and Associates Accountancy. Mrs. Groom's daughter, Ms. Michelle Groom is seen in this image below.

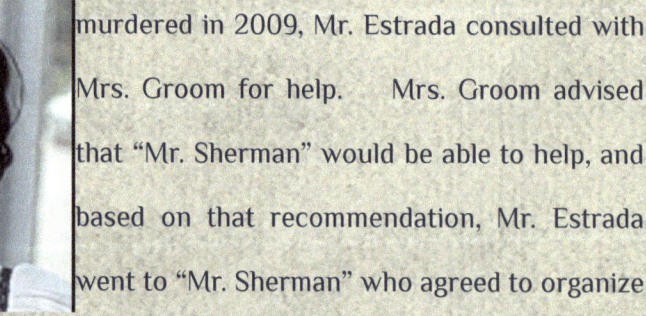

The resemblance is close, but they are not the same person. Mr. Estrada was employed by Mrs. Groom and after his partner Mr. Michael Goss was murdered in 2009, Mr. Estrada consulted with Mrs. Groom for help. Mrs. Groom advised that "Mr. Sherman" would be able to help, and based on that recommendation, Mr. Estrada went to "Mr. Sherman" who agreed to organize a civil lawsuit against Mrs. Cindy Hensley McCain for the damages he has suffered. Instead of helping Mr. Estrada, "Mr. Sherman" created collusion which compromised his legal statutes for filing a claim against and based on those actions, Mr. Estrada believes Mr. Williams may have been a victim of a homicide because if Mr Williams and Mr. Sherman were the same individual then he may have been the only ally Mr. Estrada had in this tangled web of deception and cruel intentions.

Based on the evidence presented, Mr. Estrada hereby alleges Mrs. Cindy Hensley McCain for the death of Mr. Robin Williams and pursuant to California Penal Code, an investigation is lawful and warranted to determine

- The underlying causes leading to Mr. Williams suicide
- Whether or not he was murdered to appear as if he committed suicide
- To determine if this tragedy was committed in direct retaliation against Mr. Estrada in his rightful claim for justice under the laws of the State of California

Letter to Chapman University

Professor Doti,

The Leatherby Libraries banned a nonfiction book I authored and published in 2012. To add insult to injury, the notification was sent and received on the first day of the National Banned Books week. Please understand, my book is a personal memoir about the 2009 homicide of a Los Angeles film producer. The Los Angeles District Attorney has censored this murder, and the FBI might be involved in what seems to be a full fledged and very real conspiracy. My book shares a personal testimony, bound by penalty of perjury under California State law. My case is an active legal matter pending in a California Superior Court. Social corruption forced me to expose my information and because of it, I have been targeted with extreme retaliation. However, I do not expect you to care about my misfortune. Nonetheless, you should be made aware of this situation because by acting on behalf of the university, the Leatherby Libraries' decision to ban my publication incriminates the Chapman community for acting as accomplice to the crimes being committed by the County of Los Angeles; which also implicates the university for treason since the allegation involves the murdering of private citizens, by foreign actors of hostile States, for monetary gain.

Kindly be reminded that as a leading institute of higher learning, Chapman University sets the example for social responsibility, Unless I have been misinformed, those who are privy to a crime become indirectly guilty of said crimes, by making the choice to ignore the crimes in question. Unless there has been a misunderstanding, I expected slightly better treatment as an Alum, especially when the only thing I wanted was acknowledgment.

Perhaps I should be grateful my book was not treated like rubbish and thrown in the trash instead. Whichever the case, please accept the enclosed copy of my book.. If the university wants to be an enemy to justice, then when society is demanding public accountability, Chapman University can explain how one of the privileges to a six figure education is by the mistreatment and degradation of alumni, whose circumstances do not fit the Chapman University brand or the quintessential image of its Product.

Regards, A. Estrada

Letters to Wikipedia Foundation

FROM: ALEX E.
TO: INFO-EN-Q@WIKIMEDIA.ORG
DATE: SAT, MAY 24, 2014 AT 8:57 PM
SUBJECT: BIOGRAPHIES LIVING PERSONS DEFAMATORY INFORMATION
MAILED-BY: GMAIL.COM

The Wikipedia page for Alejandro Estrada is inaccurate and the information listed is fraudulent, libelous and defamatory. In addition, the sources cited are bogus, unreliable and appear to have been manipulated by an individual acting with criminal intent because I, am Alejandro Estrada, and I am not "monkey doctor." I am also involved with an active legal matter pending in a California Court.

LOS ANGELES SUPERIOR COURT CASE NUMBER: BP115442 GOSS, MICHAEL R. - TRUST DTD 02/13/09 FILING DATE: 12/09/2009
LOS ANGELES SUPERIOR COURT CASE NUMBER: BP119874 GOSS, MICHAEL R. - DECEDENT FILING DATE: 03/11/2009

There is also an active Federal investigation into America's Help Center and I am a witness in that investigation. The disinformation provided on Wikipedia slanders my credibility because when someone tries to verify my information, the data found on Wikipedia contradicts factual information thereby creating confusion surrounding the details of the crimes in question. Therefore, by maintaining these inaccuracies, Wikipedia may or may not be contributing to the crimes being investigated by the FBI. The illogically stubborn tenacity of Wikipedia in attacking factual information and replacing it with disinformation suggests a motive for protecting the criminals targeting me and diluting my name in the media via second party news sources.

It is one thing, when a group of individuals act in orchestra to manipulate how information is presented, in order to deceive the public, and it is an entirely different thing, when a victim of a crime seeks retribution for their damages. From my understanding, a victim has the legal right not to be misrepresented with inaccurate information about them. Therefore I am asking Wikipedia to remove this page OR correct the information. If Wikipedia wants to remain neutral, then it would be in Wikipedia's best legal interest to create an article about me in order to address any deliberate and/or malicious disambiguation.

For the record, I was born in 1978. I am a Psychologist not a monkey doctor. I received my undergraduate degree from Chapman University in 2000. *Pandora, her Box and her Daddy's Curse* was published in 2012 and was republished in 2013 as *Alejandro Carbajal Estrada*. The reason

I am so high-profile is because in 2009, music artist *Lady Gaga* released the song *Alejandro*, of which I was the subject. The meaning behind the lyrics of *Alejandro* continue to be covered up with convoluted information. These efforts are tactics used in retaliation against me and the effect creates chaos and ultimately obstructs justice. According to the record, the page for *Alejandro Estrada* was created by *Primatesmx* which is not a valid Wikipedia user, yet, somehow, through some kind of magik, this user violently monitors their information, suggesting a violation of Wikipedia's policies because from my understanding, it is against Wikipedia's terms and conditions for individuals to create pages about themselves.

According to the Library of Congress as of 5/20/2014 these entries could not be found:

- Frugivores and seed dispersal / edited by Alejandro Estrada and Theodore H. Fleming. (Registration Number / Date: TX0002136090 / 1987-08-17)
- New perspectives in study of Mesoamerican primates : distribution, ecology, behavior and conservation / edited by Alejandro Estrada, Paul A. Garber, Mary S. M. Pavelka, LeAndra Luecke (Registration Number / Date: TX0006316037 / 2006-02-17)

This discrepancy was brought to Wikipedia's attention on 5/23/2014 and in fact, the only reliable records for *Alejandro Estrada* belong to me, which could explain a motive by Wikipedia because when the page for *Alejandro Estrada* was created, I had not yet become a notable person. That has since changed and the reason I have become a notable person is because I blew the whistle on the Sandy Hook massacre, two months prior. If Wikipedia and other sources had not been censoring my information, perhaps the public would have been notified with enough time to have prevented those children from being murdered.

The copyright records to my books confirm this information. I may be a prophet, but I will never be a monkey doctor. Needless to say, it is strange how in over 5 years no one editing this page has been able to provide an image of *Alejandro Estrada*, especially considering the amount of exposure I have in the media.

So, with all that said, if the *Library of Congress* records have changed in any way, then it would establish a reason to subpoena the appropriate records, in order to audit the change logs to identity the individual, or individuals, with the authority to manipulate that data. Please, kindly understand, I take this matter PERSONAL and although I am only a layperson, I would have to say that changing data in order to cover up crime might be considered an admission of guilt because on this level, doing so would be the equivalent to a Watergate scandal.

Regards,
Alejandro "Alex" Carbajal Estrada
aka. Alex Estrada, Alex Carbajal, ACE, and any other variation of the name Alejandro Carbajal Estrada

To clarify, I am not seeking publicity in any way and I would rather have the page deleted because it benefits no one. All I want is to protect my legal property, and my legal name is the only thing that has not and cannot be taken from me. My name is also my brand, Trademark and company and no one else but me, has the rights to use it.

Wikipedia Support Team
(Quality items) <info-en-q@wikimedia.org>
May 27

Dear Alex E.,

The article "Alejandro Estrada" on Wikipedia is in fact about a Mexican primatologist, who apparently meets the scholarly and/or academic notability guidelines for inclusion:

- <HTTPS://EN.WIKIPEDIA.ORG/WIKI/WIKIPEDIA:SCHOLAR>

If you feel you meet the general notability guidelines as detailed here:

- <HTTPS://EN.WIKIPEDIA.ORG/WIKI/WIKIPEDIA:BIO>

Then you may use the Articles for Creation service to submit an entry about yourself:

- <HTTPS://EN.WIKIPEDIA.ORG/WIKI/WIKIPEDIA:AFC>

We discourage people from writing about themselves because of concerns with neutrality and conflict of interest:

- <HTTPS://EN.WIKIPEDIA.ORG/WIKI/WIKIPEDIA:COI>

If your biography is accepted, the reviewer will create what we call a "disambiguation page" that lists two or more articles with the same name. Until then however, we cannot simply turn the existing article into a biography about someone else.

Yours sincerely, Kosten Frosch.

LETTER TO WIKIPEDIA LEGAL DEPARTMENT
ALEX E. MAY 28 TO LEGAL, WIKIMEDIA
HI KOSTEN,

Thank you for your quick response. Please be advised, I have elevated this matter to the Central Intelligence Agency along with supporting evidence because I am alleging Wikipedia for creating disinformation in order to cover-up criminal activity. Whether or not "Alejandro Estrada" exists is neither here nor there because the reality is I have not met him; Chances are, you have not met him either. Google puts him at the top of search results only because of Wikipedia and there is no other information on this individual else where. There are more questions about him than there are answers and what I do know, is that I am involved with a federal investigation surrounding a conspiracy to commit murder and possible domestic terrorism involving mortgage fraud and money laundering schemes and am a victim of targeting. Based on my experience, I am able to tell you that the Information Technology sector is a hot spot for criminal activity. The challenge of operating in a paperless society is that the paper trail has become electronic thereby making it much easier to delete and the change logs are nearly impossible to audit because one has to know exactly where to find the evidence.

A L E J A N D R O

It is my understanding that

> On April 9, 2009, the Wikimedia Foundation's Board of Trustees passed a resolution regarding Wikimedia's handling of material about living persons. It noted that there are problems with some BLPs being overly promotional in tone, being vandalized, and containing errors and smears. The Foundation urges that special attention be paid to neutrality and verifiability regarding living persons; that human dignity and personal privacy be taken into account, especially in articles of ephemeral or marginal interest; that new technical mechanisms be investigated for assessing edits that affect living people; and that anyone who has a complaint about how they are described on the project's websites be treated with patience, kindness, and respect. Especially in articles of ephemeral or marginal interest; that new technical mechanisms be investigated for assessing edits that affect living people

There is a reason behind everything I do and the reason I brought public attention to the discrepancy of the missing entries for *Alejandro Estrada's* copyright records was to illustrate domestic terrorism because my action caused someone to change the information on the *Library of Congress* database. Whoever that we, they must be working for Wikipedia because that cause and effect is illegal. With that said, it is strange how according to Wikipedia the article is considering low importance yet someone finds it important enough to violently monitor regularly. It would be horribly unfortunate if members of the Wikipedia community were making the assumption *Alejandro Estrada* is the individual presented solely based on the fact that he has a Wikipedia article because the physical evidence suggests otherwise.

You people, as in all the ignorant under-educated sophomoric idiot-savants working in Information Technology, make me sick to my stomach the way you know absolutely nothing, yet believe your second hand knowledge is omnipotent. Real people do not convolute their professional credibility with fake academic sources. For the fucking record, academic publications are ALWAYS

<u>A   L   W   A   Y   S</u>

published by academic sources. Such as, universities; not Limited Liability or Media Corporations, for Christ sake. *Junk Publishers* is NOT an academic or literary source. Neither is *Business Media Incorporated*. Your legal department should be able to explain to you how that fact alone makes the entire worthless article, fraudulent. It would be interesting now, to see if the *Library of Congress* records change again in some way.

If that *Alejandro Estrada* existed, then I would have already been able to sue him for the misappropriate use of my legal name and for violating my legal right to publicity. My legal name is my property. It is my celebrity and no one else but me, has a legal right to use it.

It's people like you, working at places like Wikipedia that is the reason our society is plagued by corruption and if you assholes would take your heads out of each other's asses , you might vomit from the inertia of the tail spin our country is currently in.

In fact, it almost seems deliberate.

-Alejandro Carbajal Estrada

Acknowledgments

A VERY BIG THANK YOU TO THE DEVIANTART.COM COMMUNITY AND ALL THE ARTISTS THAT HAVE CONTRIBUTED TO THE ART WORK IN THIS PUBLICATION. A VERY SPECIAL THANK YOU TO THE COPYRIGHT OWNER OF THE IMAGE USED ON THE COVER. TO VIEW MORE OF THEIR WORKS, VISIT MY PAGE UNDER THE USER NAME "IBIZA78" ON WWW.DEVIANTART.COM.

ALEJANDRO

HAVE YOU SEEN EITHER OF THESE YOUNG MEN?

Both of these young men disappeared while delivering the Des Moines Sunday Register. John Gosch has been missing since Sept. 5, 1982. Eugene Martin disappeared on Aug. 12, 1984. If you have information concerning either boy call the Des Moines, Iowa, Police Department Hotline
COLLECT 515-246-9988.

John Gosch was 12 years old when he disappeared on Sept. 5, 1982, while delivering newspapers in West Des Moines, Iowa. He was described as 5 feet, 7 inches tall, weighing 140 pounds, with blue eyes and light brown hair.

Eugene Martin of Des Moines, Ia is 13 years old and disappeared on Aug. 12, 1984. He is 5 feet 3, 105 pounds, thin, with dark brown hair, brown eyes and a dark complexion. He was wearing blue jeans, a gray midriff shirt with white stripes and red sleeves, and blue Trax tennis shoes with white diagonal stripes.

$94,000 REWARD

$25,000 offered by The Des Moines Register for information leading to the recovery of either of these missing persons. (Additional reward money being offered by businesses, friends and relatives.)

...ael Aquino (in uniform), then-editor of the Church of Satan journal The Cloven Hoof, and his wife Lilith atten...ion with Ray Harryhausen (seated on couch, left), George Pal (center on couch) and FJA's assistant Dennis B... Photo taken circa 1970.

"Yes, many people will die when the New World is established, but it will be a much better wo... those who survive." - Henry Kissinger

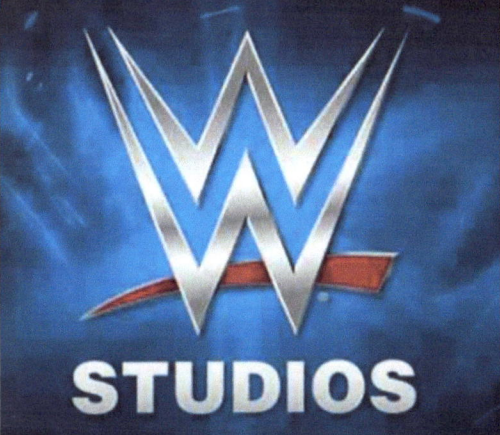

GOVERNOR BROWN INSIDER FILED FALSE DOCUMENTS, CONCEALED HUNDREDS OF THOUSANDS OF DOLLARS IN 'DARK MONEY CORPORATION'

Deputy Legislative Secretary Martha Guzman-Aceves, her boss Legislative Secretary Gareth Elliott, California Secretary of Labor David Lanier, and other employees appointed by Governor Brown also violated state law and the Governor's own Conflict of Interest Policy by failing to turn over complete and accurate financial disclosure records to the Fair Political Practices Act as required by statute.

His Mother was Bilhah, a maidservant to Rachel, another one of Jacob's wives. Genesis records his birth as 1737 B.C.

LUST CAN BE COSTLY
IT NEVER COMES FREE

It has been prophesised antichrist will have a father from the Dan and a mother from tribe of judah.

Blood makes you related

Loyalty makes you family

Afterword

Two cents, and change

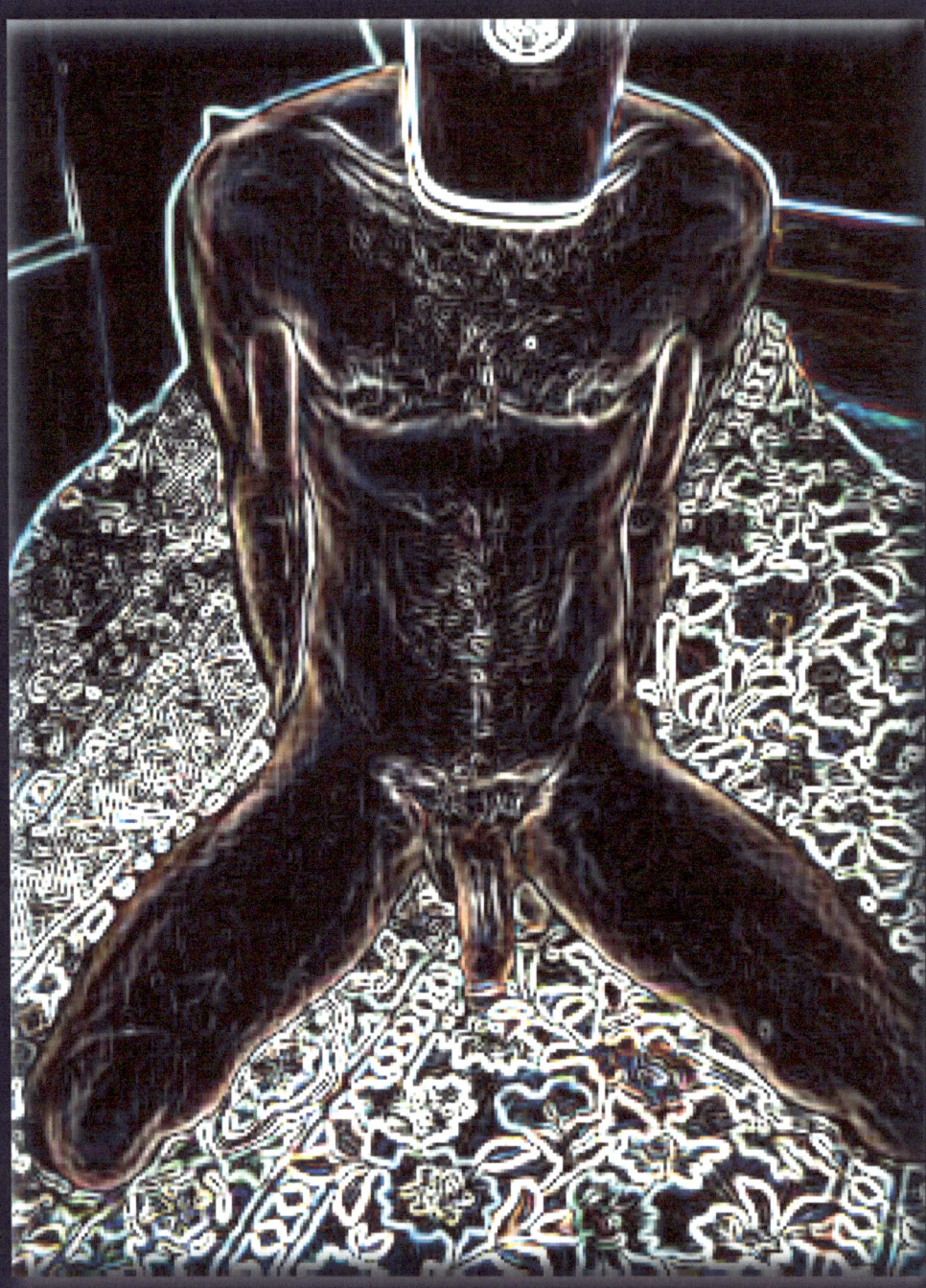

It is now 2 years after the original book was published and I believe, I have been successful with uncovering 95% of the truth regarding the Conspiracy to murder Michael Goss.

I now know that Colonel Michael Aquino, MD was the mastermind behind the military Psych-Op implemented to throw off my investigation. That piece of information was the missing link that finally completes the puzzle and ties everything together. It makes complete sense now. The ties to government. The social corruption and links to local authorities. The meetings Michael Aquino had at the Santa Ana Police Department. The pickups and drop offs at the Federal Building in Santa Ana, California. The building at 1515 N. Main Street and the underground tunnels that connected it to the Civic Center complex. The classified technology that was used to manipulate the GPS tracking by placing that building in "Uluru." The cult-like chanting I would hear through the office wall followed by the sound of people begging for their lives. Noises that will haunt me for the rest of my life. All of it, finally makes sense.

The organized killing that Michael Aquino orchestrated was brilliantly executed. There were no loose ends and the entire machine ran flawlessly. That was, until I came into the picture. Michael Aquino's decision to target gay men was the secret to it's success and it made his enterprise fantastically wealthy. In fact, despite how greedy Michael Aquino became, the seditious conspiracy continued to bulldoze its way through the Justice Department.

Doctors, as a rule, are the most corruptible sector of society. The entire scheme relied on the network of physicians that Cecy Groom organized in addition to the medical corporations that provide home health care and own numerous nursing homes throughout Southern California. These corporations reported 3 times as many employees as they really employed and their quarterly revenue was in the millions. In addition to the estate assets acquired from the elderly victims they target.

According to Michael Aquino, the patients are given fatal doses of what he referred to as a "Beta Blocker." This drug is injected, like insulin, and it causes the heart to stop. Then it is metabolized and does not show up in toxicology. There is a network of funeral homes that cremate the deceased victims and the hospital records are manipulated to enhance the legitimacy of the death, except when requested, the hospital is unable to produce the transfer documents between the hospital and the Mortuary listed on the record. Sometimes, like in the case of Michael Goss, the Mortuary address does not exist. When I filed a claim with the State of California's Board of Mortuaries and Funeral Homes, I was advised by the investigator than she had been given an order to abandon the case, which she disclosed to me during a recorded interview.

The physicians and lawyers are blackmailed with child pornography. This is the reason I believe the age of consent must be abolished. According to our law, children under the age of consent have no right to say "No." This is a Human Rights violation which contributes to child exploitation. The Law is not intended to function as a moral compass. In fact, Law cannot judge morality because Law is amoral. Moreover, there is a separation between Church and State which makes it illegal for the State to enforce laws based on a perception of morality. In addition, age of consent laws are a violation of privacy and they are used by the State to force its jurisdiction into the private lives of private citizens. Age of consent laws do not protect anyone because these laws prohibit children from having the right to "Say No." Essentially, age of consent laws treat children as property at the mercy of their adult guardian. Considering the fact that 70% of reported child abuse cases are perpetrated by a parent of guardian, these laws only put children in danger.

If every person regardless of age, had the right to "Say No," then the entire underground network of child exploitation would vanish because these law, were written by sexual predators, for the purpose of protecting their crimes. Furthermore, when a law forbids a person from engaging in behavior that is viewed as immoral, it becomes oppression. For instance, in the United States, there was a time when the law forbad non-white citizens from engaging in municipal life because racial integration was perceived as immoral.   In turn, when the State prosecutes based on an underage violation, the Law acts as if the child had been raped, without a proper psychological inquiry to determine if, in fact, the child had been raped. As a psychologist, my understanding of child development allows me to view the situation from a child's perspective.

During cognitive development, a child's understanding of the world around them is based on a sense of touch. Therefore, a child associates good with everything that feels good and bad, with everything that feel bad. Boys are, by nature, more aware of this because of their penis, which feels good.

The problem arises because we live in a female dominated society in which male sexuality is demoralized and emasculated. A child does not have the cognition to understand this social complexity and cannot comprehend the reason their society believes their penis is bad. As a result, the boy begins to develop a secret misogyny that he may never even realize he has.

The effect from this, is a lack of respect for women and that forms a rape culture because it is the only way the boy knows how to assert his power in order to regain his sexual dominance.

Ultimately, the reason these laws damage society is because judgement is passed on someone, for doing something that everyone, essentially does. As a result, the State creates the victims from innocent children without the basic human right to have their own voice while ignoring the real victims of childhood rape.

Unfortunately, at this current stage, our society cannot be repaired. In 2012, we had a chance but sadly, my voice was snuffed and my message was ridiculed. Nevertheless, I made one last, and final attempt last month, when I gave Col. Michael Aquino a directive to organize his military network to support my initiative in bringing Treason charges against the Clinton regime, by force through military action. My desperation is caused by the immediate future facing this country. I am a Prophet and Messenger of G-D and a true descendant of the House of David. My ancestors have been among the greatest monarchs to have graced humanity and I have the natural power and divine guidance to create peace on this earth and ensure justice to every soul alive, except my hands are tied in shackles by the Global Elite. The one man with the influence required to provide the infrastructure needed to eradicate this modern form of slavery, is too scared of me to follow his destiny. Rightfully so, because I do not forget.

It is ironic, how Michael Aquino spent his entire adult life looking for me, and it was I, who found him. Yet he failed to recognize me and now avoids facing me like a coward. As if, ignoring me, has ever been beneficial to anyone.

ACE

dated 9 August 2016

The truly unfortunate thing, for the future of human kind, is how, for the first time in human history, we have the power to win a revolution without spilling innocent blood and losing innocent lives; yet, no one is willing to lead that fight.

The United States of America has become an institution for modern slavery. Perhaps, this vision was the original concept when England gave her colonies Independence. However, We the People, are our military and the Armed Forces of the United States has an obligation and legal duty to protect the People from a tyrannical government; NOT to enforce imperial dominance over other foreign sovereign States.

It would be treasonous for any commanding officer in the military to undermine the rule of law by using the power of his position against the benefit of the People.

The solution would be achieved by revoking power from anyone abusing power, eliminating outstanding credit, refunding consumers the amount of interest they have paid to banks, arresting the Global elite and confiscating their liquid assets in order to distribute equally among every human being. By destroying the banks, we can recover our economy.

As easily as hitting no more than five keys on a computer keyboard. "They" are terrified of the day you realize it, wake up, and then press those keys.

That time, is now.

www.ingramcontent.com/pod-product-compliance
Lightning Source LLC
Chambersburg PA
CBHW041608220426
43667CB00001B/5